ENGLISH POLITICS IN EARLY VIRGINIA HISTORY

Alexander Brown, D.C.L.

Author of "The Genesis of the United States"
"The Cabells and their Kin" and
"The First Republic in America"

HERITAGE BOOKS
2012

HERITAGE BOOKS
AN IMPRINT OF HERITAGE BOOKS, INC.

Books, CDs, and more—Worldwide

For our listing of thousands of titles see our website
at
www.HeritageBooks.com

A Facsimile Reprint
Published 2012 by
HERITAGE BOOKS, INC.
Publishing Division
100 Railroad Ave. #104
Westminster, Maryland 21157

Copyright © 1901 Alexander Brown

Originally published
Boston and New York:
Houghton, Mifflin and Company
The Riverside Press, Cambridge
1901

— Publisher's Notice —
In reprints such as this, it is often not possible to remove blemishes from the original. We feel the contents of this book warrant its reissue despite these blemishes and hope you will agree and read it with pleasure.

International Standard Book Numbers
Paperbound: 978-0-7884-2611-7
Clothbound: 978-0-7884-9222-8

DEDICATION

This book is most respectfully inscribed to those citizens of the Republic who wish to render historic justice to the Patriots who instituted the popular course of government in this country.

         ALEXANDER BROWN.
NORWOOD P. O.,
NELSON COUNTY, VIRGINIA.

CONTENTS

PART I

An outline of the primary effort of the Patriot party in England to plant a popular course of government in America, and of the Court party to prevent it; showing that a great historic wrong was done our patriotic founders by James I. and his officials in the evidences preserved by and licensed by the crown, and why it was done   1

I. Introduction   3
II. Obtaining the first (1609) charter   6
III. Inaugurating the movement 13
IV. Obtaining the second (1612) charter, etc. 21
V. Inaugurating the government 26
VI. The controversy becomes a contest 30
VII. The first appeal to Parliament 35
VIII. The continued contest 42
IX. The second appeal to Parliament 49
X. The charters annulled 52

PART II

An outline of the effort of the Court party in England to obliterate the true history of the origin of this nation; showing how a great historic wrong was done our patriotic founders by James I., his commissioned officials, and licensed historians 57

I. The crown confiscates the evidences 59
II. The effort to preserve the evidences 69
III. The history licensed by the crown 73

PART III

An outline of the contest over our political and historic rights between the Court and Patriot parties, from 1625 until the Patriots determined to secure their political rights by force of arms in 1776; showing the ways by which the original historic wrong was supported and perpetuated under the crown   87

CONTENTS

I. Under Charles I., 1625–1641 89
II. Civil war, 1641–1646 104
III. Parliament, etc., 1646–1660 107
IV. Of the control over histories 108
V. Notes from 1660 to 1746 116
VI. Stith's History of Virginia 124
VII. The records of 1619–1624 133
VIII. Under George III., 1760–1776 140
IX. Of boundary rights 147

PART IV

An outline of what has been done both towards perpetuating and towards correcting the historic wrong since the loyal political point of view was reversed in 1776 . . . 151
I. Thomas Jefferson as a laborer in the field of original research 153
II. Jefferson's "Notes on Virginia" 158
III. History under the influence of past politics, 1784–1861 164
IV. Past history under the influence of present politics . 170
V. An explanation of my work in this field, 1876–1900 . 178

PART V

A review of some of the leading political features in the case between the Patriot party, which managed the business and laid the foundation upon which this great nation has been erected, and the Court party, which controlled the evidences and laid the foundation upon which the history of this great movement has been written . . . 191
I. Of the movement 193
II. Of the charters 204
III. Of the corporation 216
IV. Of the forms of government 228
V. Of the managers, etc. 236
VI. Of the motive, — *vis vitæ* 245
VII. Conclusion 249

INDEX 263

PART I

An outline of the primary effort of the Patriot party in England to plant a popular course of government in America, and of the Court party to prevent it; showing that a great historic wrong was done our patriotic founders by James I. and his officials in the evidences preserved by and licensed by the crown, and why it was done.

CHAPTER I

INTRODUCTORY

THE case of our patriotic founders, because of the results which have naturally followed the complete control over evidences held by their opponents, has been misrepresented for over two hundred and fifty years, and has come to be so entirely misunderstood that it cannot be corrected suddenly.

All issues naturally produce opposing evidences, and tend to obscure facts; but of all influences, not one has had a more absolute effect under monarchies in the past, on the history of reform movements, than politics. Policies of government were even more vigorously censored than matters pertaining to religion. The absolute authority possessed by the opponents of such movements enabled them to obliterate the truth of the history as performed from the pages of the history as published to such an extent that contemporary "histories" of such movements have frequently really reversed the true view of history; given the honors to those to whom they were not due; censured those who deserved praise, and conveyed ideas of the whole movement which were agreeable to those who opposed its reform features, but were unfair to the reformers promoting those features.

While the laborer in the field of original research in pursuit of the truth must find it very difficult to discover sufficient impartial and authentic evidence on which to base the true history of any movement which fell under the ban of those who opposed the movement and controlled the evidences, it is not necessary for him to labor entirely in the dark. " Authority springs from reason, not reason from authority — true reason need not be confirmed by any authority." He must be guided by the light of reason. And reason shows that unless the press is free a licensed history is obliged to conform to the purposes of those who control the press; that the more inspired by interdicted liberal ideas a movement was, the greater was the necessity for the royalist censors opposing those ideas to obliterate the historic facts regarding them permanently; that the greater the difficulty in finding facts is in itself a circumstantial evidence of the especial importance of the facts which have been concealed; and that the positive effort to suppress authentic records is sufficient evidence in itself against those making the effort to condemn any " history " which was published under their auspices, even if no counter evidence at all can be found.

The controversy over the accuracy of Smith's history has been called "the John Smith controversy," because Smith was regarded as the responsible author of the book; but the real controversy, the real case, was between the Patriot party, which determined to plant a popular course of government in the New World, and the Court party, which opposed that purpose. The object of this book is to explain this case and the results of this controversy; to show that the political principles involved in the contest between the two parties were of vast importance to us, and to give due consideration to the influence of politics on our earliest history.

I will first give an outline of the political importance of the primal movement [1] under which a popular course of government was inaugurated in our country; showing that an historic wrong was done our patriotic founders by James I., his commissioned officials, and licensed historians — both in the evidences of the Court party preserved by the crown and in the histories licensed under the crown. And this outline will also show why this wrong was committed.

[1] I will explain more fully the leading political features of the movement in Part V.

CHAPTER II

OBTAINING THE CHARTER FOR THE ORIGINAL
BODY POLITIC, 1609

IT is necessary to note the royal charter signed by James I. in April, 1606, and to outline the enterprise as conducted thereunder; but it must also be noted that this enterprise was not of a popular political character — the political features were under the control of the crown. In this charter James I. claimed all of America between 34° and 45° north latitude, which was then called Virginia, for the crown, and granted limited plantations under certain conditions to two companies. To the company for the first colony was given the privilege of making a plantation between 34° and 41° north latitude, the bounds of which, however, were confined to the limits within one hundred miles of the seacoast, and within fifty miles each way northward and southward of the "seating place," after that place was settled upon. The companies had the privilege of sending over some of the king's subjects to secure these areas of land; but the king reserved to himself the right to furnish the form of government for the companies in England and plantations in America, and also to appoint the officials to execute the same, both in America and in England: the plantations and companies being really directly under the political control of the crown, while the members of the companies paid the expenses, stimulated by the hope of finding gold mines, or a passage to the South Sea, or some present profit.

Under the form of government furnished by James I. for the plantations, the members of his council in America had the right of suffrage among themselves; but they were representatives of an absolute king. The planters had no control over them, and little or no part in the government, which was imperial; being based on the king's principles of despotism, it gave the people (the body politic) no political power.

In December, 1606, the first fleet for the first, or South Virginia, colony sailed under the charter of April, 1606, at the expense of the company, but under the orders of the king's council *for* Virginia in England, with a sealed box containing commissions for those appointed to the king's council *in* Virginia, and with instructions, etc., to them from James I. himself. The fleet arrived in Virginia in May (N. S.), 1607, when the box was opened, the commissions issued, and the king's form of government was inaugurated in Virginia, and so continued until it was necessary to alter it in order to save the colony.

While the king's form of government for the

colonies was in force in Virginia during 1607–1610,[1] important foreign and domestic, religious and political policies were developing in England, which were destined to shape the future of North America. Among these, in order to understand the case, it is very important to consider especially:—

First. The controversies with Spain, and, at this time, with especial reference to the case of The Richard (which had been captured by Spaniards while *en route* to North Virginia), then before Parliament, with Sir Edwin Sandys as "the chairman of the committee on Spanish wrongs."

Second. The religious controversies, following the Hampton Court Conference.

Third. The political controversies, which I propose to consider in this book.

In these political controversies we will find on the one side "the men of genius and enlarged minds," who were then adopting the principles of liberty, forming themselves into a political party, variously called the Patriot, or Liberal, or Independent party, "advocates of English rights," "opponents of the secret court Spanish party," etc. At the head of this party or political element was Sir Edwin Sandys, whom James I. came to regard as his "greatest enemy," as "a crafty man with ambitious designs," etc. Gardiner says: "At this time, toleration in the

[1] See *The First Republic in America*, pp. 21–119.

church and reform in the state were the noble objects of Sir Francis Bacon, and next to him no man enjoyed the confidence of the Commons more than Sir Edwin Sandys." He had aided Bacon in drawing up, "with great force of reasoning and spirit of liberty," the celebrated remonstrance of the Commons to the conduct of James I. towards his first Parliament. On the other side, we find the members of the Court party, advocates of imperialism, becoming more and more active in opposing and in trying to suppress the growth of the principles of liberty, and in disseminating their ideas of the virtues of "the kingly power," contending that it descended directly from God. This party was under the leadership of James I. himself, who had already published his "True Law of Free Monarchies," his "Basilikon Doron," his "Premonition to all most mighty Monarchs," and other such like imperial dogmas, and had already sent both to North and to South Virginia what the Court party called "His Majesties most prudent and Princelye form of government."

In the midst of these budding political controversies several planters — including Gabriel Archer, who had already proposed to have a parliament in Virginia — arrived in England with the breath of "the free air" of America inspiring them, and also with unfavorable reports of the condition of affairs in Virginia, amounting really to an acknowledgment that the enterprise had failed under the king's form of government, and that without some vital incentive to proceed the enterprise must be abandoned. Many of the patriots, who were "loudly groaning" under the same sort of government in England, were already interested in the American movement, and the reports of these planters naturally appealed to them. After consultation with the planters and after considering among themselves the unpromising outlook of their own political case in England, the inspiration came to them " to lay hold on Virginia as a providence cast before them of double advantage," — of escaping the tyranny of imperial government, and of establishing, as a refuge, a more free government in America. They determined to try to secure from James I. a charter erecting them into a corporation and body politic; conveying to that body in perpetuity a definite portion of the Spanish West Indies; granting to that body the privilege of establishing therein a government of their own making modeled on the English constitution as construed in the most favorable way to them. From the date of this determination the actual settlement of North America by the English became a reform movement of an ever-increasing political importance, and a factor in the political issues then beginning between the Court party (the crown) and the Patriot party (the people).

Had the enterprise been successful under the king's government, it would have been folly to petition James I. for a charter to a body politic; but the plantation had really failed, some of the company had already given it up, many others were anxious to give it up, and the unpromising outlook was unquestionably instrumental in inducing James I. himself to give up his cherished royal prerogatives and to grant the far-reaching privileges petitioned for to a body politic (planters and adventurers) in perpetuity. There was no other alternative. North Virginia had already failed under his form of government; and if he had attempted to continue his government and refused to grant the charter of 1609, it is evident that South Virginia would have been abandoned by the English and the destiny of North America would have passed into other hands and been shaped to other ends.

The petition for the charter to a body politic was drafted in the winter of 1608–1609 by Sir Edwin Sandys, and the charter itself was prepared for the king's signature by Sir Francis Bacon and Sir Henry Hobart. This charter (and the subsequent charter of 1612) was so drafted by Sandys that many of the prerogatives formerly reserved by James I. in his charter of 1606 were granted to, or would finally pass to, this body politic, together with the authority to institute other enlarged and liberalized rights in perpetuity; the corporation forming virtually a primitive state in its political capacity, which was really designed to be the generator of the people whom it was proposed should become in the course of time the proprietors of the boundary granted between 34° and 40° north latitude, extending from ocean to ocean, and who should receive the benefits accruing under these charter rights as fully as they now do.

It must be noted, especially, that James I. did not actually possess a foot of land in the large territory granted, and that he did not bind the crown to procure the land for the body politic. The great American wilderness in which the patriots proposed "to erect a free popular state," — the first republic in America, — whose inhabitants were to have "no government putt upon them but by their own consente," — was thousands of miles away across the vast ocean, inhabited by wild Indians, and claimed by the crown of Spain. The body politic had to acquire the land from these owners and claimants by purchase, by diplomacy, or by force, and to settle it — all "at the expense of their own blood and treasure, unassisted by the crown of Great Britain." And, of course, this had to be done before the proposed political purposes could be properly inaugurated therein. The acquiring and settlement of the lands granted could only be attained with sufficient pain, peril, and expense justly to entitle the body politic to the liberal charter rights granted by the crown in perpetuity. And it was for the sake of these rights, undaunted by the terrors of the Atlantic, by the power of Spain, by the climate and savages of Virginia, — in the face of every difficulty, disaster, and political opposition, — that the true foundation of this nation was laid. "Give me Liberty or give me death!" was the inspiration of our foundation as well as the battle-cry of our Revolution.

CHAPTER III

INAUGURATING THE REFORM MOVEMENT

THE first charter to our original body politic was finally signed by James I. on June 2, 1609.[1] It inspired the enterprise with a new life. The managers of the business at once shouldered their responsibilities and undertook their task most earnestly. Of course they did not set forth publicly the political policies which were inspiring them; but at one of the meetings of the well-affected promoters of the enterprise (after the petition was sent in, but before the charter was signed) Robert Johnson delivered a discourse touching their intended project, which was

[1] For the reasons given in *The First Republic in America*, preface, pp. xxiii, xxiv, I shall use the present style dates.

printed in February, 1609, under the title of *Nova Britannia,* which gives an outline of their business purposes, and, with the present understanding of the case, throws some light on their political purposes also.

It is important to note that Sir Thomas Smythe was constituted the first treasurer of the corporation; because, having been imprisoned for the part taken by him in the rising of the Earl of Essex in the time of Elizabeth, he was then regarded as "*a good patriot.*" This event was an incident in the rising of the popular spirit, that had become more pronounced in England when the patriotic men of genius turned their eyes upon America "as a providence cast before them" for setting on foot their reform ideas in the New World; but those who controlled the evidences were against Essex, and therefore the truth regarding the incident may never be known. It is known, however, that many of the old friends of Essex became actively interested in the American movement.

It has been well said that "when the founders of the colonies came over, it was a time of general tyranny both in church and state throughout their mother island," and church and state were so closely allied that it is somewhat hard to treat of religion and politics separately; so although I am not dealing with the religious questions, it is important to call attention to the following facts, as they throw needed light on the politics or policy of this movement. February 27, 1609, soon after James I. had replied favorably to the petition for the new charter, letters were written to the Plymouth people to become members of the body politic before the charter was signed, and many of them did so. On June 9th, only seven days after the charter was signed by the king, the Earl of Southampton, the Earl of Pembroke, Robert Sidney Lord Lisle, Thomas West Lord De la Warr, Sir Thomas Smythe, Sir Robert Mansfield, Sir Thomas Gates (all old friends of Sidney and Essex), and others sent a diplomatically worded invitation to "His Majesties subjects in the Free States of the United Provinces" (the Pilgrims?) offering them in an English colony in America the place of refuge which they were seeking in the Netherlands. Stith, in his history of Virginia (p. 76), says: 'Many Puritans took the resolution of settling themselves in Virginia; but Archbishop Bancroft, finding that they were preparing in great numbers to depart, obtained a proclamation from the king forbidding any to go without his Majesty's express leave.'

Many in England, however, had been prompt to avail themselves of the new charter rights, and had already embarked for Virginia in the first expedition. And pilgrims of all lands, of all creeds, and of all politics, have found refuge under those charter rights in the "sweet land of liberty," the "land of the pilgrims' pride," from that day to this.

The first fleet sent out under this charter sailed from Plymouth, England, on June 12, 1609. On the way the celebrated tempest, with 'the roaring waves which cared not for the name of king,' was encountered, and "the king's ship" was wrecked, but the American talisman — our first constitution containing the germ of our popular course of government — was on board and "not a hair perished." It is interesting to note that in Shakespeare's Tempest, the leading spirit — Ariel — protecting the fleet is doing so to secure freedom. As the Earl of Southampton was so actively engaged in this enterprise, it may be supposed that Shakespeare himself, although not a member of the corporation, was a patriot, and took an active interest in the enterprise of his old patron.

Sir Thomas Gates and Sir George Somers sailed from "the still-vex'd Bermoothes" on their new-built barks, The Deliverance and The Patience, on "calm seas," and with "auspicious gales" arrived in Virginia and cast anchor before Jamestown on the first anniversary of the signing of the first charter to the original of the body politic of this nation, June 2 (N. S.), 1610. On landing, Governor Sir Thomas Gates found the colony in a most deplorable condition. Taking with him the official copy of the new charter and his own commission thereunder, he went into the church; caused the bell to be rung; gathered the old and the new planters together; heard a zealous and sorrowful prayer by the Rev. Richard Buck, and after service caused William Strachey, the secretary, to read his commission as governor; Captain George Percy (the president of the king's council under the king's form of government) then delivered up to Governor Gates the old royal commissions, the official copy of the royal charter of April, 1606, and the seal of the king's council in Virginia. The imperial form of government designed for the colonies by James I. ended; the new charter rights went into effect; the political management of the colony passed in a measure from the crown to the "body politic," and the first step was taken on American soil in the movement inaugurated by the men of genius and enlarged minds who were then adopting the principles of liberty against monarchy, and in favor of a reform government in the New World.

This was one of the most important political events in our history, and the scene in the church at Jamestown must have been most impressive. There were present about sixty old planters, including Captains George Percy, John Martin, Nathaniel Powell, Daniel Tucker, Thomas Graves, and others who had been councilors or officials under the king's government. About one hundred and thirty-five new planters, including the Rev. Mr. Buck, the minister; Sir Thomas Gates, the governor; Sir George Somers, admiral; Captain Christopher Newport, vice-admiral, with some of his sailors; Stephen Hopkins (afterwards one of the Pilgrim fathers), with other nonconformists; William Strachey, Ralph Hamor, William Pierce, John Rolfe, and other leading men; Mrs. John Rolfe, with other women and several children; probably some friendly or spying Indians; and the guard over the proceedings was "Sir Thomas Gates his company of old soldiers trained up in the Netherlands," under the command of Captain George Yeardley.

As the Rev. Mr. Buck had brought over, "for the benefit and use of the colony," printed copies of the first sermon preached before the body politic, it may be naturally inferred that he read in his services during this historic ceremony at least the *prophetic* text of this sermon: —

"*For the Lord had said unto Abram, Get thee out of thy country, and from thy kindred, and from thy father's house, unto the land that I will shew thee.*

"*And I will make of thee a great nation, and will bless thee, and make thy name great, and thou shalt be a blessing.*

"*I will bless them also that bless thee, and curse them that curse thee, and in thee shall all the families of the earth be blessed.*"[1]

[1] *The Genesis of the United States*, pp. 283, 287.

Sir Thomas Gates, who had been chosen as the first governor of Virginia under the corporation, and other members of his military company, may have served in the Netherlands under William the Silent, the great leader of the advocates of the rights of man; and all of the company had quite certainly served under his son, Maurice of Nassau, who, like his father, was inspired by the same liberal ideas which were henceforth to furnish the sustaining influence of the English-American plantations.

A portion of the fleet which reached Virginia in August, 1609, had returned to England in the fall, filled with nothing but letters of discouragement relative to the condition of affairs in Virginia at that time. To offset these discouraging reports the managers had published in December, 1609, a broadside,[1] and soon after " A True and Sincere declaration of the purpose and ends of the Plantation begun in Virginia," [2] in which they boldly give the king's "forme of government" as one of " the rootes " of the past "defailements," and state their intention of altering it.

Thomas West, Lord De la Warr, who had been commissioned in February, 1610, as lord-governor and captain-general of Virginia for life under the new charter, sailed from England in April, and arrived at Point Comfort, Virginia, on

[1] *The Genesis of the United States*, pp. 354–356.
[2] *Ibid.* pp. 337–353.

June 16th following. Sir Thomas Gates, who had arrived only fourteen days before with his shipwrecked people from the Bermudas, had found the old planters reduced to such an exhausted state under the king's form of government that it appeared necessary to leave the country, at least temporarily, and on June 17, 1610, Jamestown was abandoned. But the providence which had protected the American talisman through "lightning and tempest" did not forsake it in "plague, pestilence, and famine." On the next day, Captain Edward Brewster (of Lord De la Warr's military company, which had served Maurice of Nassau, and, it may be, William the Silent) met the departing colonists at Mulberry Island with orders from the lord-governor, who had so providentially arrived, for Sir Thomas Gates "to bear up the helm and return to Jamestown, where all of his men relanded that night;" but Gates himself, in a boat, proceeded downward to meet his lordship, who, making all speed up, arrived at Jamestown on Sunday, June 20, 1610. In the afternoon of that day, Lord De la Warr went ashore with Sir Ferdinando Wenman and others, landing at the south gate of the palisade fronting the river, Sir Thomas Gates causing his company in arms, under Captain George Yeardley, to stand in order and make a guard to receive him. As soon as the lord-governor landed he fell upon his knees before them all, and on the bank of the James River made a long and silent prayer to God. Then, arising, he marched up into the town, William Strachey acting on this especial occasion as color-bearer, bowing the colors before him as he entered the gate of Jamestown, and let them fall at his lordship's feet, who, passing on, went into the church, where he heard a sermon by Rev. Richard Buck, and, after service, caused his ensign, Anthony Scott, to read his commission, upon which Sir Thomas Gates delivered up to his lordship " his owne commission, both patents [the old and new charters, 1606 and 1609], and the Counsell's seale." And the permanent settlement of this country by the English definitely began under the reform movement of the original of the body politic of this nation.

CHAPTER IV

OBTAINING THE SECOND CHARTER OF OUR ORIGINAL BODY POLITIC, ETC., 1610-1616

GATES and Newport sailed from Virginia on July 25, 1610, and arrived in England in September following, bringing the news of the discovery of the Bermudas. The managers of the movement then petitioned for another charter, which would include those islands within their bounds, and which would convey to the body politic other privileges which they had found to be desirable.

This petition was also drafted by Sir Edwin Sandys, and the charter was drawn up by Sir Francis Bacon and Sir Henry Hobart.

The petition was granted in the autumn of 1610, but the opposition of the Court party, which was then taking definite shape, caused delay, and the charter was not signed by James I. until March 22, 1612. The importance of understanding everything pertaining to the charters of 1609 and 1612 incorporating the embryo of a body politic, which would naturally develop in the course of time into a state in its political capacity, cannot be overestimated. The obtaining of these primal charters of our system of government was the most important political event in our history.

James I. wished to increase his dominions, but he was not willing to risk his royal revenues in settling plantations in America. In 1606 he had authorized some of his subjects to settle in those parts at their own expense; but he was a most earnest advocate of every royal prerogative, and he reserved to himself the right of governing them and their enterprises according to his own ideas. Companies of adventurers had undertaken the task with the object of reimbursing them-

selves for their outlay by finding a passage to
the Pacific Ocean, or by discovering gold mines,
or other enterprises of present profit; but before
the beginning of 1609 their hopes had generally
faded away, while the difficulties, dangers, and
expenses of the undertaking had become most
evident. It was not to the interest of these men
to carry on this work, even with a fair prospect
of success, unless they could better their condition or the condition of their posterity thereby.
The original commercial objects had been so far
from being realized that it was necessary for
some vital influence to inspire the enterprise in
order to enable it to succeed. Even if the advocates of the king's form of government were
willing to continue to prosecute the enterprise at
their own expense under the government of
James I., of course those among the adventurers
who were then beginning to breathe the principles of liberty did not wish to secure the country
at the expense of their own blood and treasure,
if there was to be established in that country
thus secured by them a form of government
which they regarded as an absolute tyranny.
But after considering the state of the case these
men became inspired with the needed *vis vitæ*,
and resolved, if they were permitted to secure
a large definite boundary and to establish therein
for the future good of posterity a reform government " conforming with the English constitu-

tion," as construed in the most favorable way to them, that they would then undertake the task and willingly carry it on, even if they did have to do so solely at the expense of their own blood and treasure.

The leading purposes of the charters petitioned for were to incorporate a body politic and enable that body to take the government of the movement from James I.; and the desire to establish in America a reform government as a refuge from the tyranny obtaining in England became the leading incentive of the enterprise.

Of course the charters were open to all parties, and members of both national political parties were included in our original body politic; but the movement was under the administration of the Patriot party from 1609 to 1624, and the enterprise was carried 'forward during that time under the management of those who held to the right ends declared.' Those not animated by the inspiring desire soon began to drop out, to fail to pay their dues, etc., and some became critics of the patriotic managers, and active opponents of their plan for protecting in the New World "the liberty of the subject from the encroachment of the crown;" while those under the sustaining influence continued to advance their purposes to the projected ends regardless of adverse criticism and all sorts of opposition, even when in doing so they were obliged to face king, council, and courts, at the risk of imprisonment and sudden death.

The reformers from the first were evidently fully aware of the great importance of the charter rights which they had now obtained. As stated in "The New Life of Virginia," they regarded the movement as 'a work of such consequence as for many important reasons it must never be forsaken,' although at the same time they well knew that there were "manifold difficulties, crosses, and disasters" to be met and overcome before "the most excellent things" which they were aiming at could be secured.

The ultimate political objects were properly held in a state of abeyance during the period of the first joint stock, 1609–1616, when the country was being secured from the Indians and Spaniards; and the colony was being planted entirely at the joint expense of the corporation, and being made sufficiently strong to enable it to stand the shock of opposition when it came. And the Patriots must have felt that it was coming (as it did come) as soon as the political objects became apparent to the crown.

I have dealt very fully with the case during this period both in "The Genesis of the United States" and in "The First Republic in America," and must refer those who may wish to have a more extended account to those books. The idea of a liberal government for America developed during the most remarkable transition period in English history, and although this idea was bitterly opposed by James I. and the Court party, it received the support of some of the greatest patriots, business men, statesmen, politicians, soldiers, sailors, and most broadminded churchmen of that period.

CHAPTER V

INAUGURATING THE REFORM GOVERNMENT IN AMERICA, 1616–1619

JAMES I. had been crowned king when he was less than fourteen months old; had been a king ever since he could remember, and regarded the right of kings to rule absolutely as being next under God. In 1616 he wrote "A Remonstrance of the most gratious King James I. for the Rights of Kings, and the independence of their Crownes;" and in the same year began to show his hand against the freedom of action of the managers by having certain royal features inserted in Captain John Martin's patent[1] for lands in Virginia, thus opportunely placing the managers of the movement on their guard before the end of the first joint stock. They had been

[1] See *The Virginia Magazine of History and Biography*, vol. vii. pp. 269–275.

obliged to use diplomacy from the first, but this act served a good turn by causing them to act with additional circumspection at a most important turning point in their movement.

The end of the absolute joint stock period (Dec. 1616) found a portion of the country apparently secured from the Indians and Spaniards and the colony quite well established. The citizens of this country were then to be given under their charter their fixed property rights in the soil, and every man's portion was to be confirmed " as a state of inheritance to him and his heyers forever, with bounds and under the Companies seale, to be holden of his Maiestie, as of his Manour of East Greenwich, in Socage Tenure and not in Capite." Early in 1617 Captain Samuel Argall was sent as deputy governor of Virginia, with special commissioners and a special surveyor, to carry out these designs. There had already been settled a laudable form of government for the courts of the body politic which were held at the capital in London. After the people were given their fixed property rights in Virginia, it became necessary for the managers to " bend their cares to the settling of a laudable form of government in the colony." With this object in view they chose Sir Edwin Sandys, who had drafted their charters, as an assistant to Sir Thomas Smith, for the especial purpose of superintending the inauguration of the original political designs in America. The intent was to establish one equal and uniform kind of government over all Virginia, such as may be to the greatest benefit and comfort of the people, in which they were to have a hand in the governing of themselves; in which they were to be eased forever of all taxes, public burthens, etc., as much as may be; in which they were to have no government, taxes, etc., put upon them but by their own consents, etc., etc.

The London house of Sir Edwin Sandys, where the consultations over the form of government for Virginia were generally held, was near Aldersgate, — the gate through which James I. first entered London, in 1603; and it is interesting to note that this gate was being rebuilt by the crown as a monument to the royal government of James I. at the same time that the plans for a reform government for our nation were being developed in sight of the gate by Sir Edwin Sandys, in consultation with the Earl of Southampton, John Selden, the Ferrars, John White, and others. There was a figure of James I. in high relief over the arch of the gate. On the eastern side were these lines: "Then shall enter into the gates of this city Kings and Princes; sitting upon the throne of David, riding in chariots and on horses, they and their Princes, the men of Judah, and the inhabitants of Jerusalem, and this city shall remain for ever."

On the western side were these lines: "And Samuel said unto all Israel, Behold, I have hearkened unto your voice in all that you said unto me, and have made a KING over you." On the southern side was a bas-relief of James in his royal robes.

Some of the plans of the patriots for the reform government in Virginia were probably embodied in the instructions and commissions sent to the colony by Lord De la Warr in April, 1618; but he died *en route*. The documents sent by him have not been found, but others, possibly of a similar character, — instructions, a constitution, and the American *Magna Charta* (so called, but it was not so great as the charters of 1609 and 1612, from which it derived its authority), — were ratified by the Virginia court in London, November 28, 1618, and carried to the colony by Sir George Yeardley in January, 1619. The authority for these instruments was derived from the charters to "the body politic," and under the authority of these instruments there was inaugurated at Jamestown in August following "the first example of a domestic parliament to regulate the internal concerns of this country, which was afterwards cherished throughout America as the dearest birthright of freemen."[1]

[1] See *The Green Bag*, vol. v. p. 216; *The Virginia Magazine of History and Biography*, vol. vii. pp. 270, 271, and *The First Republic in America*, pp. 313–323, 456.

CHAPTER VI

THE CONTROVERSY BETWEEN THE COURT AND THE PATRIOT PARTIES BECOMES AN OPEN CONTEST OVER THE REFORM MOVEMENT

At the Virginia Court on May 8, 1619, Sir Thomas Smith retired and Sir Edwin Sandys succeeded him as treasurer, and Mr. John Ferrar succeeded Alderman Robert Johnson as deputy treasurer of the corporation. It had come to pass that the loyalty of Sir Thomas Smith and Alderman Johnson to the Patriot party was doubted, and soon after this we find them affiliating with the Court party, aiding that party in their political purposes, and obscuring rather than throwing light upon the patriotic purposes of their own administration of the corporation from 1609 to 1619.

The Spanish ministers to England, Zuñiga and Velasco, from 1606 to 1613 had continually opposed the settlement of the English in territory claimed by Spain, even to urging the Spanish king to remove the colonists by force of arms. The celebrated Count Gondomar arrived in England as ambassador from Spain in August, 1613, and at first pursued a similar course; but having put his spies at work looking into the Virginia business, he became convinced, prior to December, 1616: *First*, that the English would never yield to such opposition and threatening; *second*, that some deep political scheme was animating the Virginia courts. He then altered his diplomatic plans for suppressing the colony, and began to work on the tenderest spot in the mind of James I. He assured the English king that there were deep politicians in the Virginia Company with farther designs than a tobacco plantation; " that though they might have a fair pretence for their meetings, yet he would find in the end that the Virginia Court in London would prove a seminary for a seditious Parliament." James I. was assured that " *the matter was too high and great for private men to manage;* that it was therefore proper for him to take it into his own hands, and to govern and order it both at home and abroad according to his own will and pleasure." This politic line of argument had the effect desired. The progress of the colony under the inspiration of free ideas over difficulties which hitherto had been insurmountable had already alarmed James I., and he now determined to put an end to the popular course of the Virginia Corporation. With that object in view, he resolved that Sir Edwin Sandys should not be continued as treasurer or manager of that body politic, and requested the Easter Quarter Court

(May 27, 1620) " to make choice of Sir Thomas Smythe, Sir Thomas Roe, Mr. Alderman Johnson, or Mr. Maurice Abbott, and *no other*." When this request was presented by Mr. Robert Kirkham, one of the clerks of the signet, the earls of Pembroke and Southampton told the court that this was " the beginning of a move against the company's just freedom of election, granted by letters patent " — one of their charter rights. The body politic was not willing to yield to the king's request and thus to " suffer a great breach unto their privilege of free election." They determined to defer their election to the next quarter court, and appointed a committee to wait upon the king about the matter. On May 29 the committee (H. Wriothesly Earl of Southampton, J. Hay Viscount Doncaster, William Lord Cavendish, Edmond Lord Sheffield, Sir John Danvers, Sir Nicholas Tufton, Sir Lawrence Hide, Mr. Christopher Brooke, Mr. Edward Herbert, Mr. Thomas Gibbs, Mr. Thomas Keightley, and Mr. William Cranmer) met at Southampton House, and drafted an answer to the king's request for the election of one of those selected by himself as treasurer of the corporation. When this answer was presented to James I. at his chambers, notwithstanding the fact that it was couched in the most loyal terms, notwithstanding all argument, the king " remained obstinately excepting against the person of Sir

Edwin Sandys, declaring him to be his greatest enemy, and that he could hardly think well of whomsoever was his friend — and all this in a furious passion, returning the committee no other answer but *choose the Devil if you will, but not Sir Edwin Sandys.*"

When Sir John Danvers, a few weeks later, asked the Earl of Southampton if he would accept the place if the company chose him treasurer at their next quarter court, he replied, " I know the king will be angry at it, but so the expectation of this pious and glorious work may be encouraged, let the company do with me what they please." The next court on July 8, 1620, reasserted their right to free election, and elected the Earl of Southampton as treasurer, with the understanding that Sandys should continue his services ' in prosecuting still those political ways which might give satisfaction to the patriotic undertakers.'

So far from these open controversies with the king having had a depressing effect at this time on the resolution of the managers, Arthur Wodenoth says that ' the public asserting of their charter rights at the Easter Quarter Court, at the meeting of the committee with James I., and at the Trinity Term (July 8) Quarter Court much raised the spirits of the Patriot party in the Virginia Company.'

In order to prevent confusion in the mind of

students of these premises it must be explained that there were parties in the corporation with different opinions regarding business matters, tobacco contracts, the magazine, etc., but I have given an outline of the growth of these parties in " The First Republic in America," [1] and we are not now considering these questions. The political issues of, and over, the body politic with which we are now dealing were really between the national Court and Patriot parties, and should not be confused with the party issues in the corporation, although these strictly company parties may have from time to time in the advancement of their purposes affiliated with one or the other of the national parties to such an extent as to make it, sometimes, very hard to draw the party lines accurately.

The Virginia Court of July 17, 1620, appointed several committees for perfecting the form of government which was being established in the colony: The committee to select from the laws of England such as were suitable laws for the colony was composed of Sir Thomas Roe, Mr. Christopher Brooke, Mr. John Selden, Mr. Edward Herbert, and Mr. Philip Jermyn; to select from the charters, instructions, orders, etc., and the Acts of Assembly in the colony such laws as were fit to be made permanent was composed of Sir Edwin Sandys, Sir John Dan-

[1] See pp. 244, 267, 268, 280, 289, 301, 305–307, and 398.

vers, Mr. John Wroth, and Mr. Samuel Wrote; to select from the municipal governments of the cities in England a model government for the incorporations in the colony was composed of Mr. Robert Heath, Mr. Robert Smith, Mr. Nicholas Ferrar, Mr. William Cranmer, and Mr. George Chambers. A portion of the labors of these committees will be found embodied in the documents taken to the colony by Sir Francis Wyatt in the summer of 1621.

CHAPTER VII

FIRST EFFORT TO PROTECT THE CHARTER RIGHTS BY ACT OF PARLIAMENT

PARLIAMENT had always been looked to as the friend of the movement, and both the first and second parliaments of James I. had been appealed to in that behalf.[1] Knowing that Gondomar had been ferreting out their political objects and impressing his views on the mind of James I., the Patriot party in the body politic now felt the need for strengthening and protecting their political charter rights. About November 20, 1620, it was resolved "for some important reasons" to obtain a new charter, and on November 25th the Virginia Court determined to try to

[1] See *The First Republic in America*, pp. 14–17, 20, 75, 122, 200, 215, 216.

have further privileges and immunities inserted, and also to have the charter confirmed by act of Parliament. Sandys, Southampton, Selden, Edward Herbert, John Ferrar, and probably others, were employed in drafting this new charter.

The third Parliament of James I. met February 9, 1621; Sir Edwin Sandys was a member for Sandwich, but he did not attend during the first week, and his brother, Sir Samuel Sandys, in explaining his absence, stated that 'he was interested in drawing a patent about the Virginia business, and asked the House of Commons to excuse him till that business was over.'

On March 4, 1621, Sir Edwin presented the draft of the new patent to the Virginia Court, which approved of it, determined to have it confirmed by act of Parliament, and a letter was sent to James I. about it. "The draught of the new charter" was soon presented by Sir Edwin Sandys, Edward Herbert, Esq., and Mr. John Ferrar to Attorney-General Coventry for him to prepare the charter therefrom for the king's signature; but he at once found fault with it (he may have been instructed to do so), and refused to draw up the instrument without a special warrant from James I. In April, 1621, James Hay Lord Doncaster presented a petition from the corporation to the king for this special warrant, and the matter was considered by the Privy Council in May; but I have found no evidence that the warrant asked for was ever sent to the attorney-general, or that the charter was ever presented to Parliament for confirmation by act.

In the spring of 1621, James Marquess of Hamilton and William Herbert Earl of Pembroke, two liberal noblemen, solemnly affirmed to the Earl of Southampton that they had heard Gondomar say to James I. "that it was time for him to look to the Virginia courts which were kept at the Ferrars' house, where too many of his nobility and gentry resorted to accompany the popular Lord Southampton and the dangerous Sandys."

The king was evidently determined to put a stop to the proceeding before Parliament with the proposed new charter, and had probably made up his mind to put a stop to the whole Virginia business. In view of the alliance between Prince Charles and the Infanta, diplomatically proposed by Gondomar, the king is said to have resolved to surrender unto Spain Virginia and the Bermudas, to annul the colonization charters, and to quit altogether the Spanish West Indies (America). The Patriots in our original body politic were aware of these purposes, and attributed them to "a secret Court-Spanish party" under the influence of Gondomar; but they were not willing to yield their rights. There were many Patriots in the House of Commons, and with their aid the Patriots in the Virginia

Corporation, as we have seen, were trying to forestall James I. in these his intentions by making their charter rights as secure as they could by having them confirmed by act of Parliament, when, on June 14th, James I. prorogued the Parliament to November 30th, and on June 26th (during vacation) had Southampton, Sandys, and Selden arrested. This arrest of a member of the House of Lords and of a member of the House of Commons during recess was a breach of the privileges of Parliament and an evidence of the desperate purposes of the crown. It caused a great commotion, and James I. felt it advisable to issue a proclamation to the effect that Sandys was not restrained for his acts in Parliament, but for other personal matters. John Ferrar and Arthur Wodenoth both say that it was the business of the Virginia charters which caused the arrests.

They are said to have been released on July 28th, but, although released from arrest, Sandys was restrained to his house in Kent. When Parliament reassembled on November 30th the matter was at once taken in hand by the House. Mr. Mallory soon rose and said — in the abbreviated wording of the Commons Journal — "*misseth Sir Edwin Sandys. Moveth we may know what is become of him.*"

On December 11th the Commons appointed Sir Peter Hayman and Sir James Mallory a committee to go into Kent and "see what state Sir Edwin Sandys is in, and if he is sick, indeed, to return his answer, whether he were committed and examined about anything done in Parliament, or about any Parliamentary Business."

In indorsing this motion Sir George Moore, who had contributed over $3500 to the American movement, said: "Any one was unworthy to live who would betray the privileges of this House. This our principal Freedom. Never in all his Time [he had been a member since 1584] knew greater care to preserve their Liberties than this Assembly."

On December 28th, the Commons, in reply to the king's letter, wrote the memorable protestation, in which they assert that "every member of the House hath, and of right ought to have, freedom of speech," etc., which was afterwards torn from the Commons Journal by the king and with his own hands destroyed; but I have given an outline of these proceedings in "The First Republic in America," and it is not necessary to repeat.

The party which was trying to protect the charter rights of our primal body politic [1] by act of Parliament had now become so strong that the counter purposes of the Court party could not be carried out even by an absolute

[1] Of the members of our original body politic about 300 were also at different times members of the House of Commons.

king, without some pretense of justice. This party contained some of the most influential men in England, there was a very strong following among the people, some prestige even in the House of Lords, and an ever-increasing authority in the House of Commons. And this Parliament to which they wished to appeal in behalf of their charter rights was a most vigorous one — alike in the correction of abuses and in the defense of liberties. Therefore the conduct of James I. in the case was constantly diplomatic. He had found it necessary for his purposes to prorogue the session; to arrest Sandys and others; then to apologize. And there was some prospect of success with the Virginia business if the Patriots had been able to get their case before the House; but the king dissolved it, and thus the charter act was not permitted to pass the Parliament.

The period of this Parliament should be carefully considered in these premises, as it was evidently a most important one in the history of the movement which gave birth to this nation. It was during these political proceedings of so far reaching importance to the Anglo-Saxon race that the committees of the body conducting that movement were preparing the laws for the reform government establishing in Virginia, and it was on August 3, 1621, that the Virginia Court (the "Seminary of Sedition" of James I.) signed and sealed duplicates of the ordinance and constitution which had been prepared to be sent to Virginia by the recently elected governor, Sir Francis Wyatt. The intent of the managers of the body politic was, "by the divine assistance, to settle in Virginia such a form of government as may be to the greatest benefit and comfort of the people, and whereby all injustice, grievances, and oppression may be prevented and kept off as much as possible from the said colony."

Besides the charter case there was another important case, in these premises, before this Parliament. In the summer of 1618 Captain John Bargrave brought suit against Sir Thomas Smith and others. The case went through the Virginia courts; then into chancery; then before this Parliament; and (after Parliament was dissolved) before the Privy Council. During this controversy Bargrave repeatedly warned the royal courts against "the popular government" which was being instituted under the popular charters, and constantly urged them to take prompt and vigorous steps for tying Virginia to the crown of England.

CHAPTER VIII

THE CONTINUED CONTEST BETWEEN THE COURT AND PATRIOT PARTIES OVER OUR CHARTER RIGHTS

COUNT GONDOMAR, having apparently succeeded in his mission, left England for Spain in May, 1622, and James I., in carrying forward his intentions against our charter rights, proceeded with discretion. He sent a very polite message to the Virginia Easter Court (June 1, 1622) "signifying that although it was not his desire to *infringe their liberty of free election,* yet it would be pleasing unto him if they made choice for Treasurer" from five merchants whom he mentions;[1] which message the Virginia Court — meeting diplomacy with diplomacy — pretended to regard as "a full remonstrance of his Majesty's well-wishing unto the plantation, and *of his gracious meaning not to infringe the priviledges of the company, and the liberty of their free elections;*" and thereupon proceeding with their election they gave the Patriot candidate, the Earl of Southampton, 117 ballots, while the king's candidates received only 20 votes in all. The Virginia Court then requested William Lord Cav-

[1] See *The First Republic in America*, p. 476.

endish, William Lord Paget, and John Holles Lord Houghton 'to present their most humble thanks to his Majesty for *his good wishes to their affairs without desire to infringe their liberty of free election,*' etc. When the committee presented this really sarcastic message, James I., very naturally, "flung himself away in a furious passion," and Prince Charles had to act as a peacemaker.

The Patriots never hesitated in contending for our charter rights at any time, and at the Virginia courts during this period they did not hesitate to assert that James I. was acting in the matter in the interest of Spain, under the influence of Gondomar. And even the Court party must have felt the need of proceeding with diplomacy, for although James I. was "an absolute king," the Patriot party was using a club which then had great force in England. But when the news of the massacre of the Virginians by the Indians reached England late in June, 1622, the Court party, attributing that incident to "misgovernment" (that is, to the popular course of government), seized upon it as furnishing the desired excuse for suppressing the movement, and the Patriots were obliged to use, if possible, greater discretion than ever, until the good reports brought from Virginia by the ships which arrived about Christmas, 1622, put them on the aggressive again.

Early in 1623 " A Declaration of the present state of Virginia comparatively with what had been done in former times" was drawn up and set forth by the order of the Earl of Southampton, then treasurer of the corporation. The officials of the "former times" were now acting with the Court party. Alderman Johnson replied to this declaration at once, and the Virginia Corporation was soon divided into bitter political parties. Wodenoth says that, 'owing to the constant opposition of James I. and to the inquisition of the Privy Council, many Lords and others of all ranks of the more timorous nature now fell from the true sense and justice of the work chiefly intended,' and these men formed a party in the body politic itself which aided the Court party in having the charters annulled, and the government resumed, by the crown.

The party in the corporation which was willing to surrender our charter rights to the king and affiliated with the Court party was led by Robert Rich Earl of Warwick, Sir Thomas Smith, Sir Nathaniel Rich, Sir Henry Mildmay, Alderman Johnson, and others. The party not willing to surrender our charter rights to the king, hoping, with the aid of the Patriot party in Parliament, to be able to hold on to those rights, was led by Henry Wriothesley Earl of Southampton, William Lord Cavendish, Sir Edwin Sandys, Sir Edward Sackville, Sir John

Ogle, and many more. The case, ostensibly, between these two parties in the Virginia Corporation, but really between the crown of England and the original of our body politic, was up before James I. and his Privy Council in January, February, March, and April, 1623, documents being read and witnesses heard for both sides. By the latter part of April the case had reached an acute state.

On April 22d, the Patriot party appointed Sir Edwin Sandys, Sir Edward Harwood, John Smyth of Nibley, John White (who afterwards drafted the Massachusetts charter), William Berblock, Anthony Withers, Rev. Patrick Copeland, John Ferrar, and Nicholas Ferrar as a special committee for perfecting the various writings which they intended to submit in defense of our charter rights, etc. On April 28th, the crown appointed a special commission to consider the Virginia case, with Sir William Jones, who had been chief justice of the King's Bench in Ireland, at the head of it. This commission sat in this case for many months, and back of it was James I. and his Privy Council.

John Ferrar says: " The Privy Council, finding that the company were still resolved not to part with their patent or with the liberty which they thereby had to govern their own affairs, now took a more severe and not less unjust course. They confined Lord Southampton [early in May, 1623] to his house, so that he might not come to the Virginia courts, of which he was the legal governor. But this only made the company more resolute in their own defense. They then [on May 23d] ordered Sir Edwin Sandys [Lord Cavendish, the governor of the Bermuda Islands Company, Nicholas and John Ferrar] into a similar confinement. But this step in no degree abated the resolution of the company " to defend their charter rights.

At the Easter Virginia Court, May 24, 1623, " the Lords, under the influence of Gondomar, strongly pressed the company to give up their patent;" but they would not. All of the leading managers of the body were now under arrest, and as this was the court at which their annual elections were usually held the crown may have felt that it "held the whip handle;" but the Patriots, in order to hold on to their old officers (now prisoners), and to avoid as much as possible an open rupture with the crown, determined to defer the annual election to the Trinity term. James I. was thus again foiled in another attempt to interfere with their freedom of election. The Ferrars were liberated in a few days; but Southampton, Cavendish, and Sandys were not.

On May 26th, Sir Nathaniel Rich, who was then affiliating with the Court party, had a long interview with Captain John Bargrave in the great chamber of the Earl of Warwick's house in London. Bargrave said that " by his long acquaintance with Sandys and his wayes he was induced verilie to believe that there was not any man in the world that carried a more malitious heart to the government of a Monarchie, than Sir Edwin Sandys did." Continuing, he said in effect that 'Sandys had told him his purpose was to erect a free popular state in Virginia, in which the inhabitants should have no government put upon them but by their own consent.' This evidence of Bargrave's as to the political features of the case was very strong, because he was a friend of Sandys on business lines, and was then acting in consort with him in his suits against Sir Thomas Smith. Rich made notes of this interview, which he gave in to the king's commissioners, who were then considering the case.

Sandys and Southampton being under arrest, John Ferrar says that the burthen of defending our charter rights before this commission and the Privy Council fell upon Nicholas Ferrar. And when James Marquess of Hamilton and William Herbert Earl of Pembroke visited Sandys and Southampton in their confinement, these lords informed them of these proceedings, saying: "That Nicholas Ferrar, though now left as it were alone, was too hard for all his opposers. But, continued they, your enemies will prevail at last; for let the Company do what they can, in open defiance of honour, and justice, it is absolutely determined at all events to take away your patent."

The Trinity Virginia Court met on July 5, 1623; the treasurers were still under arrest, the company would not elect others to their places, and in order to hold on to their old officers and to avoid an open rupture with the crown, now deferred the election to the Michaelmas term. James I. seems to have been determined, if the patriotic body would elect none of those selected by himself, that they should have no presiding officials at all.

The crown had placed the leaders of the Patriot party under arrest, and had hampered that party in every way while the commissioners were considering their case. After the commissioners had collected such evidences as the king desired, they made their first report in July, 1623: — to the purport 'that if his Majesty's first charter of April, 1606, and his Majesty's most prudent and princely form of government of 1606–1609, by thirteen councillors in Virginia all appointed by his Majesty, had been pursued, much better effects would have been produced than had been by the alteration thereof under the charters to a body politic into so popular a course,' etc. The report was for the purpose of justifying James I. " out of his great wisdom and depth to judgment to resume the government, and to reduce that popular form so as to make it agree with the monarchical form which was held in the rest of his Royall Monarchie."

CHAPTER IX

THE SECOND EFFORT TO PROTECT OUR CHARTER RIGHTS BY ACT OF PARLIAMENT

AFTER the failure of the Spanish match, in the autumn of 1623, James I. evidently altered the private purpose, which the Patriots said he had, of surrendering Virginia to Spain, but became more determined than ever to annul our charter rights, in order to take the country from the body which had secured it at the expense of their own blood and treasure without assistance from the crown, to attach it absolutely to the crown, and to resume the government himself.

On October 30th, the company was required by the crown to take a final vote on surrendering their charter rights voluntarily, and, regardless of the royal influence, a large majority of those present were opposed to doing so. Two of the old representatives of James I. in Virginia during 1607-1609 (Captains John Martin and John Smith) were present, and both of them wished the king to resume the business.

Sir Edwin Sandys had been under arrest nearly

the whole time since May, — while this case was being considered by the crown, — and James I., in order to get him entirely out of his way, had determined in December to send him as one of a special commission to Ireland; but a Parliament having been decided on, and Sandys being elected a member from Kent, the king was foiled, as it was deemed unwise to arouse the wrath of Parliament by taking him away from his seat; so he was finally released from confinement, and he sat in the fourth Parliament of James I. from February 22, 1624, to the death of the king on April 6, 1625.

On January 24, 1624, the Virginia Court resolved not to continue the prosecution of their case before the crown officials, the Privy Council, and courts, but "to reserve all to the Parliament now at hand;" and it was before the last Parliament of James I. that our original body politic made their last stand as an independent corporation in defense of our original charter rights. The Patriot party was numerously and well represented in this Parliament. After it met, on February 22, 1624, Sir Edwin Sandys and Nicholas Ferrar (M. P. for Lymington) at once strengthened their position by taking sides with Prince Charles and the Duke of Buckingham (who had visited Spain as Tom and John Smith), the then "rising stars," in their case against Lionel Cranfield Earl of Middlesex, the old opponent of Sandys and Ferrar in the Virginia business. Then, on May 6th, Sandys, Ferrar, and "those others of the Virginia Council that were also members of the Honourable House of Parliament," in the name of the Virginia Corporation, presented a petition " To the Honourable House of Commons assembled in Parliament." This petition, after showing the many advantages arising and likely to arise from the colony, states that disorders have arisen which the petitioners were not able to rectify "without higher assistance," and "for the discharge of the trust reposed in them they now presented to this present Parliament this child of the kingdom [Virginia] exposed as in the wilderness to extreme danger, and as it were fainting and laboring for life. And they pray the House to hear their grievances;"—which the House was willing to do, and a committee was appointed to hear the case. But before the matter was concluded James I. wrote (May 8th) "to our House of Commons not to trouble themselves with this petition," as he intended to settle the matter himself with the aid of his Privy Council, and 'this was assented to by a general silence in the House, but not without some soft mutterings.' As their contest was really with the crown, and not with the Sir Thomas Smith party, as, for obvious reasons, they had pretended, and as their hopes had been dependent on the Commons, the

Patriot party in the Virginia body politic must have now felt that their cause was for the present hopeless; yet they were not only unwilling to surrender our charter rights voluntarily, but they were not willing to surrender them at all.

CHAPTER X

THE CHARTERS TO THE ORIGINAL OF OUR BODY POLITIC ANNULLED BY THE CROWN

ON November 3, 1623, the Privy Council in England appointed Captain John Harvey, John Pory, Abraham Piersey, and Samuel Matthews[1] commissioners in Virginia to consider and make report on the condition of the colony. Harvey and Pory arrived at Jamestown on March 4, 1624, and after considering the case, sent their reports to England by Pory early in May following. The Patriot party in Virginia had sent Mr. John Pountis as their agent, with documents to offset these reports, about a week before, and this was probably the first special mission sent to England from the colony in defense of our charter rights. "Mr. Pountis, the messenger of the General Assemblie in Virginia," died *en route* at sea in June, 1624. Mr. Pory, the messenger of the royal commission, arrived safely, and gave in their reports about the middle of June. The

[1] John Jefferson was also appointed, but he did not act.

royal commission in England then, regardless of the protests of the Virginia courts in England and of the General Assembly and planters in Virginia, made their final reports justifying the king in having the charter of our original body politic annulled and in resuming the government himself.

James I. then had the charter overthrown, on June 26, 1624, by a *quo warranto*[1] in the Court of the King's Bench by Sir James Ley, who had formerly served him as a commissioner in Ireland; but the immortal principles which inspired the body had then been planted in America. The seed had germinated in our sacred soil, and the tender plant was growing strong in our free air.

The Patriot party was very severe in denouncing James I. in their courts and writings for his "despotic violation of honour and of justice" in these premises, and that the whole proceeding of the Court party was a piece of very dishonorable work there can be now no question; but from the imperial point of view it must have seemed to be a royal duty to resort to every possible means available for destroying forever, "root and branch," every idea of the popular political course of government designed for the New World by the Patriots.

In reference to the *quo warranto* case, John

---

[1] Smith called it "*A Corante*." — *Generall Historie*, p. 168, Arber's edition of Smith's Works, p. 621.

Ferrar said that Attorney-General Coventry brought the plea against the company's charter, "That it was in general an unlimited vast patent. In particular, the main inconvenience was that, by the words of the charter, the company had a power given them to carry away and transport to Virginia as many of the king's loving subjects as were desirous to go thither. And consequently, by exercising this liberty, they may in the end carry away all the king's subjects into a foreign land," etc. Additional light is thrown on this matter by Bargrave, Wodenoth, and others.

If we will turn the political light on these charters it will be seen that Attorney-General Coventry understood them correctly.[1] They conveyed to a body politic unlimited in number, a corporation unlimited in time, a vast territory in perpetuity, and authorized that body to plant this territory, not only with "as many of the king's loving subjects as were desirous to go thither," but also with 'strangers and aliens, born in any part beyond the seas wheresoever, being in amity with the English.' And among the singular freedoms, liberties, franchises, and privileges granted to the members of this body politic was the right to govern themselves — to make laws and ordinances — so always as the same be not contrary to the laws of England as construed in the most favorable manner for that body.

[1] See Part V. chapters i., ii., and iii.

The crown already saw "the handwriting on the wall," and felt that, unless heroic action was promptly taken against a popular course of government in America, the colonies would become a place of refuge from royal tyranny, and would finally shake off the yoke of the mother country and erect an entirely independent nation. And the subsequent history of the colonies is an evidence that the crown never lost sight of that fear until it lost the colonies.

After the *quo warranto* case had been decided according to his desire, James I. at once turned his attention to designing a plan of government of his own for the colonies in America, with the aid of Oliver St. John Viscount Grandison, George Lord Carew, and Arthur Lord Chichester, who had previously assisted him in forming his plan of government for Ireland; and if he had lived to put into effect his plan of government for America, the result might have been the same in this country as it has been in Ireland. Or, if Gondomar's advice continued to obtain with him, the Spanish plan of ruling South America might have been repeated in North America. Or, if he had restored his original form of government of 1606–1609, under the presidency of his original loyal representative, it might have resulted in failure as it had previously done. But no one can really know what would have been the result if the ideas of

James I. and his councilors had been completely carried out; because Providence has always protected the American talisman. James I. died suddenly on April 6, 1625, before his plans for destroying it had been consummated, and it came to pass that the colony virtually continued under the political principles — the *vis vitæ* — of the primitive body politic of this nation.

PART II

An outline of the effort of the Court party in England to obliterate the true history of the origin of this nation; showing how a great historic wrong was done our patriotic founders by James I., his commissioned officials, and licensed historians.

CHAPTER I

THE CROWN CONFISCATES THE EVIDENCES OF THE BODY POLITIC

JAMES I. not only determined to deprive the body politic of the political rights which he had granted under the Great Seal of England in perpetuity, but he also resolved to suppress (their historic rights) the real history of their great reform movement.

We have considered the means resorted to for robbing the original of our body politic of our charter rights. We have now to consider the means adopted for robbing our founders of the honors due them in history; for suppressing the facts, and for impressing on the public false ideas of this great liberalizing movement.

The repressive laws then shackling the press would of themselves have naturally worked the loss or scattering of much that was disapproved by the crown in the lapse of years without an intentional preservation of evidence for one party and the destruction of the evidence for the other side; but James I. was not the king to leave such matters to such chances, or to trust solely to the ordinary royal control over evidence. Probably no king was ever more determined to exercise "the divine right," formerly claimed by all kings, for making the historic statements controlled by them conform to their purposes, than James I. The real history of his part in the Gowrie Conspiracy of 1600 and in the Gunpowder Plot of 1605 has never been satisfactorily unraveled. But his subtle diplomacy in matters of this kind was most effectually illustrated in his determination to make the plantations in America lasting monuments of his own kingly ideas, rather than of the popular ideas of "his greatest enemy," Sir Edwin Sandys, and in the execution of his purpose to consign to oblivion all that pertained to the political plans of the Patriots and to their reform movement. We have a peculiarly strong illustration of the vigor of his purpose in these premises in his act on January 9, 1622, when, in order to destroy the record of a popular political idea, he was guilty of the historic crime of tearing out with his own royal hands the page from the Commons Journal on which was written the celebrated protest of the Commons (in sequence to the arrest of Sandys in June, 1621) asserting " that they had, and of right ought to have, freedom of speech," etc. To securing these objects — to committing this great historic wrong — James I. devoted "his great wisdom and depth of judgment," with the aid of the Court party, Privy Council, special commissioners, royal courts, licensed historians, personal advisers, dissatisfied and royalist members of the Virginia Corporation, for a large portion of the very last years of his life and reign. And consequently even the Gowrie Conspiracy and the Gunpowder Plot have been better understood by historians than has the reform movement under which this nation was founded.

The crown had a legitimate or legal right to control the press, the printed evidences, and much of the manuscript evidence — such as pertained to the acts of the crown, the Privy Council, royal courts, commissions, etc., etc. It is now hard to form even an approximate estimate as to how much there was originally of the evidence legally under the control of the crown; but there was evidently very much of it, — some of a reliable character and some of a partisan or unreliable character; some complete documents, others mere abstracts. But it was all kept under lock and key, "tied with red-tape," and none of it was available to the historian for many generations, prior to which time much had been destroyed intentionally or unintentionally, and some yielding to the natural ravages of time had crumbled to decay.

It is only necessary to give an outline of the evidences in print and manuscript, originally issued by or under the control of the Virginia Corporation. Prior to the opening of the press to their opponents in 1612, the managers of the business had published about twenty tracts, broadsides, and circular letters. After that their patronage of the press was not so free. The custom of reading at the annual Hilary term of the Virginia Quarter Court " a declaration of the present state of the colony " was continued during 1613–1617, which declaration, or an abstract from it, was published each year, and a few lottery broadsides and circular letters were also printed; but I cannot find that anything at all was published by the managers in 1618 or 1619, while the new order of government was being quietly inaugurated in Virginia. Under the Sandys-Southampton administration, " the treasurer was required in the beginning of the court [usually the Easter Quarter Court] at the giving up of his office to declare by word or writing the present estate of the colonie and planters in Virginia, and to deliver in to the court a Booke of his accounts for the year past, examined and approved under the auditors hands: Declaring withall the present estate of the cash." A portion of this report, including 'A Note of the shipping, men, provisions, etc., that had been sent to Virginia by the said Treasurer during his preceding year in office,' was published in 1620, 1621, and 1622. Besides these a good many other things were printed in 1620 and a few in 1622; but the printing press was not available to the managers in the years 1623 and 1624 when the great struggle over our charter rights was going on, and they published nothing that I can find in those years. There were probably over fifty imprints — tracts, broadsides, circulars, etc., licensed and not licensed, long and short — published by the managers in the whole period of 1609-1624. These publications, issued in the interest of the enterprise, are not expected to give political or other information which might injure it; yet they reveal to us some of the lines along which the managers worked, some of the difficulties which they had to meet, some of their objects or ideas of the present and hopes for the future, and along these lines they must be regarded as authentic evidence of the highest value. At the same time it must be remembered that the crown had a legal control over the press which printed them.

The manuscript records of the body politic were regularly kept, were voluminous and valuable. The treasurers, auditors, committees, husbands, etc., all kept separate sets of books. The bookkeeper kept the books of the treasurer and the books of the auditors. The secretary kept the books of the corporation courts, the books of the committeemen, etc., including: *First*, the books containing letters, orders, etc., from the king, Privy Council, and court officials to the company officials, and *ditto* from the company officials to the crown officials; *second,* the books of laws, standing orders, and matters of that character; *third,* the books containing the charters from the crown, the charters and indentures from the corporation, the public letters to and from Virginia, etc.; *fourth,* the books of the acts of the general courts; *fifth,* the books of the acts of the committees, including invoices of goods, etc., sent to and received from Virginia; and, *sixth,* the books containing the names of the adventurers and their shares of land, the names of all planters in Virginia upon the public as well as upon private plantations and their shares of land. There were also register books, in which the name, age, condition, previous residence, etc., of all who went to Virginia as planters was registered. The husband kept his own books regarding every voyage to and from Virginia. There were also many other writings, documents, etc., of an important character not kept in books, all of which were carefully kept under the secretary's charge in the company's chest of evidences. And, of course, there was much evidence, of a non-official but reliable character, in the hands of many members of the corporation not kept in the chest of evidences. I believe that enough is now known of these original manuscript evidences of the Virginia Corporation to justify estimating the volume at over seven million words.

The crown, through the medium of the Star

Chamber, the High Commission, and the censors of the press, had a legal control over publications, and through the Privy Council and royal officials a legitimate control of much of the manuscript evidence. But James I. was also determined to confiscate this mass of the corporation's evidence over which he had no legal control, and over which I do not know that the annulling of the charter to the body politic gave him a legitimate control. The actual confiscation of this evidence began on or before May 3, 1623, for the Virginia Court of May 24th complained that the Lords of his Majesty's Privy Council had sequestered their court books out of the company's hands three weeks before. On May 25th, the royal commissioners ordered the Virginia and the Somers Islands companies to bring before them to the inquest house (where they held their inquisitions), next adjoining to St. Andrew's Church in Holborn, on May 27th next, all writings of all sorts concerning the said companies. As the Privy Council had taken the precaution to place the presiding officers of both corporations under arrest while this sequestration of their evidences was going on, this order of the commissioners was addressed to "Edward Collingwood, secretary of the Company of Virginia."[1]

In the autumn of 1623 the crown appointed

[1] For Captain John Smith's account of his part in these proceedings, see *The Generall Historie*, pp. 162-168.

Captain John Harvey and John Pory to go to Virginia and to act with several planters there as commissioners in Virginia, ostensibly for the purpose of examining into the state of the plantations, 'to make report on the *misgovernment* thereof, and to suggest the likeliest ways to be put in practice for the better governing of the same;' but really, as Lionel Cranfield Earl of Middlesex expressed it — ' In order that we [the Court party] might have some true grounds to work upon.' That is, in plain English, the royal commissioners in England and in Virginia were appointed for the purpose of finding reasons, evidences, to justify the king before the people in annulling the popular charters, and in resuming the government himself, as he had already made up his mind to do. "There was one law of the land, but another law of the king's commissions." They collected such evidences as answered their purpose, and made their reports — regardless of the protests of the Virginia courts in England and of the General Assembly in Virginia — in accordance with the wishes of the crown.

Captain John Harvey and Mr. John Pory of the commission in Virginia were in the service of James I. Pory had been secretary in Virginia, but at the election of June, 1621, was defeated by Christopher Davison, and afterwards went over to the Court party. On July 30, 1624, 'the crown paid him £100 in discharge of his expenses, and £50 as a reward for his services when employed in Virginia about the king's special affairs.' James I. expended much more of his revenue in his effort to have evidences to conform with his wishes, in founding history to suit his ideas, and in committing this historic wrong, than he did on the actual founding of Virginia.

The commissioners continued to confiscate the company's evidences[1] at every opportunity, under various pretensions, until the Virginia charter was "overthrown" on June 26, 1624, by a *quo warranto* issued by Sir James Ley,[2] Lord Chief Justice of the King's Bench; after which James I. felt more free to act in the matter without pretext or subterfuge. On July 4th he appointed a special commission to aid him in the premises, composed of sixteen men, the large majority being crown officials or members of the Court party; and one of their first acts was to order Mr. Nicholas Ferrar, the deputy of the Virginia Corporation, to bring to them many of the company's evidences. On July 25th James I. enlarged

[1] See *The First Republic in America*, pp. 532, etc.

[2] He was created Lord Treasurer on December 20, 1624; Lord Ley of Ley, County Devon, December 31, 1624; advanced to the Earldom of Marlborough in May, 1625, and soon after made Lord President of the Privy Council, all for services rendered the crown. Sir William Jones, the head of the king's Virginia Commission of 1623–1624, was advanced to the King's Bench, October 17, 1624.

the powers of this commission, added thereto forty new members, mostly of the Court party, and gave them especial royal orders, 'to take into their hands and to keep All Bookes, orders, Letters, Advices, and other writings and things in anywise concerning the colony and plantation of Virginia, in whose hands soever the same be.' And all persons were required by the crown to deliver these evidences to these commissioners, while they were required by James I. to be diligent in securing them.

It is not to be supposed that anything in manuscript or print would have been preserved under the auspices of the crown which was not favorable to the purposes of the crown, and if the royal officials collected any evidence which did not conform to the purposes of the crown, it was probably collected in order to destroy it. The evidences still preserved which were obtained by the royal commissioners consist of extracts made in the interest of the royal purposes from documents which have not been found (having been probably destroyed at that time), and of complete papers in justification of those purposes. There cannot now be any reasonable doubt that James I. left no stone unturned in the effort to find and to have destroyed all evidences which were favorable to the popular course of government. And all the numerous important original manuscript evidences of the body politic were confiscated by the crown, with the manifest purpose of suppressing the facts and making it impossible for the truth regarding this reform movement ever to be known, for not one of these original documents has been found. And "censored histories" were licensed, disseminating false ideas, which, under the control of the crown, remained for generations the only available evidences in the premises.

Besides the official publications of the crown and of the managers, there were printed various other books, sermons, tracts, etc., by members of the corporation and by outsiders, containing more or less matter relative to the colony in Virginia. But as these publications had to conform to the purposes of the censors of the press, little information of a political or strictly reliable historical character is given in them.

CHAPTER II

THE EFFORT OF THE PATRIOTS TO PRESERVE AUTHENTIC COPIES OF THEIR EVIDENCES

WHILE the Court party had every advantage in being able to destroy evidences unfavorable to their purposes and for disseminating such as were favorable, the Patriot party was at every disadvantage. Even before the open opposition of the crown began there had been need for discretion, not only on account of the political conditions, but also because it would have been a serious blow to the enterprise for many years for many of the true obstacles to have been publicly acknowledged by the managers. Hence they had all along been obliged to bear in silence adverse criticism and charges of mismanagement as well as of "misgovernment." And although they patronized the press liberally during 1609–1612, the freedom of the press was never theirs; whatever they published was always liable to royal inspection — to be censored, garbled, or destroyed. And after the crown resolved to confiscate their evidences, they really had no safe or satisfactory way of preserving them. The only way was by stealth, and fortunately for the truth, which is essential to history, they made determined efforts to preserve their records in this way. Some were preserved by sending them to Virginia at once, others by keeping them privately in England, and some of these were at a later day purchased by Virginians and brought to Virginia for safe keeping.

The Virginia Court, on May 27, 1623, appointed a committee composed of Sir Robert Killigrew, Sir John Danvers, Edward Herbert, Richard Tomlyns, John White, Anthony Withers, John Bland, Gabriel Barber, and William Berblock to attend the royal commissioners with a portion of the evidences which they had demanded, and to ask the commissioners in the company's name that "they would respite the delivery of the accompts until the accomptant might take copies of them, when together with the other things they should be delivered to them." But we now know that the copying of the records for private preservation began before May 27, 1623.

It is now quite certain that both Sir John Danvers (so long an auditor of the company) and Mr. Nicholas Ferrar (the deputy treasurer), "foreseeing the destruction of the company's records," had copies made privately. Danvers had "The Leiger-Court Books" (the acts of the general courts, beginning with the quarter court of May 8, 1619, and ending with the court of June 17, 1624) copied and attested, and Ferrar had "all the court books and all other writings belonging to the company" copied and attested. Both the Danvers and the Ferrar copies were delivered (by Danvers and Ferrar respectively) for safe keeping to the Earl of Southampton, the last treasurer of the company, in the summer of 1624. As soon as the royal commissioners learned of these copies they called on the earl for them; but, regardless of the royal orders, he replied that "he would as soon part with the evidences of his land as with the said copies, being the evidence of his honor in that service." Southampton soon went to the

Netherlands, where he died, and James I. himself died not long after. Thus Providence, which preserved our political rights, also preserved these evidences; for it need not be supposed that any of these copies could have been preserved if James I. had lived longer. The Ferrar copies are still missing. Those which have been found are of vast importance, not only within themselves, but also in showing the character of the evidences which were then confiscated by the crown.

The absolute control over all evidence then possessed by the crown did not produce the only serious difficulty in the way of finding the facts in after times, for the control of an absolute king over the lives of his subjects made it necessary to their safety for them to conduct matters very secretly. It was not safe to keep complete records of a movement in which life and liberty were at stake, and there was constant need for diplomacy. Many acts, resolves, etc., of the Patriots were without doubt never recorded at all, and evidently much of the company's record has to be "read between the lines." Even the books of "The Seminary of Sedition" reveal so little of the political character of the corporation that the Rev. William Stith and subsequent historians, who had the use of some of these books, regarded the Virginia body politic as being merely a commercial company.

There is still another difficulty, owing to the parties which arose in the Virginia Company itself, frequently causing the evidence of one party, when relating to the acts of the other, to be unfavorable and *ex parte* evidence. Thus members of the parties in the corporation either willingly or unwittingly played into the hands of the royal commissioners by furnishing evidence the one party against the other.

CHAPTER III

THE HISTORY PUBLISHED UNDER THE AUSPICES OF THE CROWN

It was very natural for such a king as James I. to determine to efface every trace of such a movement as this was, and, unfortunately for the truth, he did not die until after the original evidences of the corporation had been confiscated, until after the censored histories had been published, and his plans against the true history of the great reform movement had been consummated.

The chief means resorted to by the crown for preventing the truth from ever being found out was by suppressing the manuscript evidences; and the chief means for perpetuating such false ideas as were agreeable to the Court party was through the censored press. Therefore, in considering the effect of politics on the history of the original of our body politic as it has been published, it is of the first importance to form a correct estimate of the original history published under the auspices of the crown, which has been the foundation upon which subsequent histories have been based. In order to do this satisfactorily, it is necessary to consider the character and position of the author; the conditions obtaining and influencing opinions and evidences when the book was compiled and when it was published; the view-point and character of the matter in the book; the circumstances which fostered the book for generations; and, finally, to note the character of the fruit which has been produced thereby. I have written a great deal about this book which it is not necessary to repeat. What I am going to write shall have reference especially to the political conditions which have not previously been sufficiently considered.

I have regarded Captain John Smith as the responsible author of this " history," and as such have held him personally responsible for its contents, character, and the historic harm which has been done by it, and I may have blamed him too much in the matter; for, save for the support of the Court party, the book would not have been licensed or published, and therefore James I. and the Court party are really more to blame for the publication of his " history " than he is himself. It is true that he criticised the managers, but so did the Court party. It is true that his personal purpose was evidently to glorify himself; but as his authority to act in Virginia and his authority to publish his stories in England were derived from the crown, both as an official in Virginia and as a historian in England he was really the servant of the crown. The references to himself being considered not personal, but in the sense of his political position as the king's loyal representative, — the honors for the services rendered by the official servant of an absolute king were thought to belong to the king his master, — therefore he was free to carry out his personal purpose completely so long as his story conformed with the purposes of the crown. If his services in Virginia had been greater even than he says they were, and if his accounts had been written in defense of the political purposes of the Patriots, they would have been suppressed by the crown as such evidences were suppressed. If he had acted with the Patriots, protested against the king's form of government for the plantations, returned to Virginia under the body politic, supported the popular course of government, upheld our charter rights, and given up his life in America while carrying forward the great cause, he would have fared in histories published under the auspices of the crown as the martyrs of our genesis did fare. History cannot be written or estimated fairly without giving due consideration to the influence of politics on the evidences.

Let us consider the conditions which led up to the publication of this book: Captain John Smith was a prisoner charged with the capital offense of complicity in "the open and confessed mutiny" of Galthorpe when he arrived in Virginia in 1607; but his life was protected by the commission which he held from James I. as a member of his council in Virginia. Under the influence of the free air of America, respect for the king's authority in Virginia soon began to wane. In January, 1608, of the six members of the king's council in Virginia, Wingfield had been deposed, Gosnold had died, Kendall had been executed, and under the leadership of Captain Gabriel Archer, who wished the planters (to whom James I. had not granted the right to govern themselves) to set up a parliament of their own in Virginia, Smith was tried for disobedience of orders, and condemned to be executed; but the coming in of Captain Christopher Newport, who held his own commission from the crown at this time, prevented the assembling of the parliament and saved the life of Smith.[1]

In December, 1608, when Captain Newport left Virginia with the planters and reports which were instrumental in causing the Patriots to petition for a charter enabling them to remove the

[1] See *The First Republic in America*, pp. 55, 56, 67.

king's council and to reform the king's plan of government in Virginia, Captain John Smith was the president of the king's council representing James I. in Virginia. In August, 1609, when the portion of the corporation's fleet arrived with the news that the charter to a body politic had been granted, Smith was not only the president, but the only surviving representative of the king in his council in Virginia. Unfortunately these ships did not bring the official copy of the new charter, as it was in charge of the governor, Sir Thomas Gates, who had been wrecked on the Bermudas; and the absence of this charter, coupled with the knowledge that it had been granted, caused a confusion of authority in Virginia. Smith, as president of the king's council, held on to the official copies of the original authorities, — the king's charter of April, 1606, his princely instructions of November, 1606, and his constitution for the plantation of March, 1607, and made the circumstances thus obtaining a pretext for refusing to admit Captains Radcliffe, Martin, and Archer (old members who had returned with the fleet) into that council, although, like Smith, they had been appointed thereto in the first instance by his majesty; whereby " discencyons " arose between the president of the king's council and these captains, Captain Francis West, and others, which finally resulted in his being deposed from the presidency and sent to England to answer for his misdemeanors.[1] Captain George Percy, who was in Virginia with Smith the whole time of his service there, said that he was an ambitious, unworthy, and vainglorious fellow; that he aimed at setting up "A Soveraigne Rule" in Virginia, and was justly deposed; but his acts in the premises were well calculated to receive the subsequent indorsation of the Court party, as they evidently did do.

The ships on which he returned to England arrived in December, 1609, with very bad reports regarding the conditions in the colony when the fleet left Virginia; but it was afterwards asserted by the Court party and in the history licensed by the crown that the colony was left in excellent condition by the loyal representative of James I., and that the bad conditions did not begin until after the ships of 1609 (which brought the bad reports from Virginia) had left Virginia, which assertion is manifestly untrue.

The royal grant of 1606 to a company had been superseded by the charter of 1609 to a body politic; but the charter had not reached Virginia. The managers in England, feeling the danger of chaos obtaining in Virginia, fitted out Lord De La Warr as soon as possible and

[1] The corporation had no authority to punish such misdemeanors until after the granting of the XIV. and XV. articles of the charter of 1612.

sent him to the colony with the authority of an absolute governor, and he arrived just in time to save the country to the corporation. Gates returned to England in September, 1610, carrying the first news of his shipwreck in the Bermudas, and subsequent arrival in Virginia, as well as of the safe arrival of Lord De La Warr, and the managers of the movement soon determined to petition for their second charter.

Captain John Smith, the king's former representative in Virginia, began to take action against the charter under which he had been removed from office in Virginia and the managers who had removed him, at his earliest opportunity. Late in 1610, at the same time that the petition drafted by Sir Edwin Sandys for this second charter was being considered by the crown, and afterwards during the period in 1610-1612, when the managers of the business were trying to fill in the charter with subscriptions to the desired amount of £30,000, — before James I. signed it, — a treatise, which had been compiled, it was said, partly in Virginia and partly in England, by some (one or more) of those who had served in the colony under the crown, and had returned to England, was being circulated in manuscript evidently under the patronage of a party opposed to the reform purposes of the Patriots. The avowed motive of this treatise was to show " to all indifferent readers, that the country was healthy, the Indians tractable," etc., the "defect whereof hath only been in the managing the businesse." In brief, the motive was to show that the reasons for "the past defailments," which the managers had assigned to justify them before the king in petitioning for the special charters incorporating a body politic, were not true. The circulation of this treatise probably delayed subscription; but the country had not yet been secured from the Indians or Spaniards, the colony was not yet established, James I. was not yet willing to risk his own revenues in the undertaking even under his own officials and plan of government, and so, regardless of this opposition, the charter was finally signed by the king on March 22, 1612.

Late in 1612, when James I. was acting as his own prime minister, and when the enterprise was passing through its "darkest hour," some of those who agreed with the political motive of the said treatise felt justified in having it published at Oxford. It was dedicated by its author, Captain John Smith, to his patron, Edward Seymour Earl of Hertford. The managers had been subjected to verbal and written criticism, to opposition and all sorts of hindrances from the beginning, and now in this dark hour the press was opened to their opponents; thenceforth they were to have still greater need for all the wisdom which their natural abilities and long experience had given them. Thenceforward their great reform movement had to be carried on in the face of the open and ever increasing opposition of the party in the state and in the church which controlled the press; opposed their political purposes, and finally confiscated their evidences and licensed the history of their enterprise as it was first published.

While their opponents of the Court party were printing at Oxford a criticism of their management and purposes, and were thus laying the narrow foundation for the false history of their great reform movement as it has been published, " God's secret purpose " to uphold the work was so strongly fixed in the minds of the undaunted managers that they were holding weekly courts at the house of Sir Thomas Smith in London, " yielding their purses, credit, and counseil, from time to time, even beyond their proportion, to uphold the plantation," and were thus preserving through " the darkest hour " the broad political foundation upon which this great nation stands erected. But most unfortunately they had no control over the press, and the subsequent accounts of their movement, licensed by the crown, were based on this *ex parte* Oxford tract.

It was immediately followed up by the first edition of " Purchas his Pilgrimage " in 1613, and the second edition of the same in 1614 ; Howes' first edition of Stow's Chronicles in 1615; the third edition of Purchas in 1617; the second edition of Howes in 1618, etc. Smith himself summarized the same ideas in his "Description of New England" in 1616, and in his "New England's Trials" of 1620 and 1622, and there were other imprints of less historical pretensions during 1613-1622, upholding the political purposes of the Oxford tract, and opposing those of the managers of the movement.

In the spring of 1623, when Sir Thomas Smith's party in the Virginia Company was contending that the colony had prospered under his management, and charging that it had gone to ruin under Sandys, etc., and the Sandys party was denying both the claim and the charge, the author of the Oxford tract began compiling a book virtually contradicting both of these parties; contending that the colony had prospered under his management and under the king's form of government, and had gone to ruin after the alteration thereof; asserting that the business had been mismanaged by Sir Thomas Smith prior to 1617, and under the administration of Sandys since that year, etc. In the following summer, Captain John Smith, the author, was before the king's commissioners, and gave such answers to seven questions as were calculated to please the Court party and to justify

James I. in his purpose to annul the charters that conveyed the political rights which have sustained this nation since its birth. Late in 1623, Smith was distributing a prospectus of his " Generall Historie of Virginia," etc., among the nobility and gentry of England, beginning: " These observations are all I have for the expences of a thousand pound and the losse of eighteene yeares of time." He then entreats them to " give me what you please towards the impression," etc. He soon found a patroness in the Duchess of Richmond and Lenox, the widow of his former patron, Edward Seymour Earl of Hertford, and also the widow of Ludovic Stuart, late lord steward of the king's household. On June 26, 1624, the charters of our body politic were overthrown in the king's bench; on July 4th, a special royal commission was appointed to aid James I. in confiscating the evidences of that body; and on July 22d, Smith's history of the enterprise of the company conducted under the crown (1606–1609), as well as of the reform political movement conducted under that body (1610–1624), was licensed by Master Doctor Goad, and entered for publication at Stationer's Hall in London.

Rev. Thomas Goad, D. D. (1576–1638), who licensed the book, was a domestic chaplain to George Abbot, Archbishop of Canterbury, head of the Privy Council, and of the High Commission, which, together with the court of the Star Chamber, had a special control over the press. As we have seen, there had been a long and bitter contest between the Court and Patriot parties over our original political charter rights, and the obtaining of this license at this time did not depend on the personal disinterestedness of the author, nor on the fairness of the book to the patriotic managers, planters, and adventurers, who had secured this country for us at the expense of their own blood and treasure unassisted by the crown, nor on its value as history; but to the contrary it depended on the loyalty of the author to the purposes of the Court party, and on the book's conforming to the purpose of James I. to obliterate the true idea of this great political movement, and to rob our patriotic founders of their historic rights and of the honors due them. The Court party wished to show the public that much better effects had been produced under his Majesty's most prudent and princely form of government than under the popular course of the Corporation,[1] and both the view-point and matter in this "history" are in accord with the purposes of James I. and the Court party.

When the Oxford tract was being printed, the faithful managers, planters, and adventurers were very earnestly trying to carry the move-

[1] See *The First Republic in America*, pp. 541, 542.

ment through its darkest hour and to save the colony at their own expense. When "the Generall Historie" was being compiled, the faithful Patriots had secured the country for us at the expense of their own blood and treasure unassisted by the crown, and were trying to defend our political charter rights against the assaults of the Court party. The publication of "the tract" marks the active beginning of the movement in favor of the king's resuming the government of the plantations, and annulling the company's charters; and the publication of "the historie" marks the culmination of that movement under James I.

"Purchas his Pilgrimes" which had been licensed in 1621, was finally published in four large volumes not long before the death of James I. The Rev. Samuel Purchas, the author or compiler of this work, as chaplain to Abbot, Archbishop of Canterbury, and head of the High Commission, had authority, as such, to examine manuscript to see that it conformed to or was loyal to the purposes of the crown, — was not seditious, — and to license books. And he was probably looked to by the Court party as *the* historian of the colonial movement;[1] but the Virginia matter in his volumes was evidently either largely based on Smith's works, or collected for him by Smith, and therefore to all in-

[1] See *The First Republic in America*, pp. 635–637.

tents and purposes Captain John Smith must be regarded as the authorized author under the crown of the history of the movement which was published under the auspices of James I. Hence the so-called "John Smith controversy" covers the published history of the period, 1606–1624, and may be more properly called the controversy between the Patriot party, which founded the country, and the Court party, which founded the history. But James I. was really the responsible author or founder of this controversy.

PART III

THE influence of politics on the historic record while the evidences continued under the control of the crown, — an outline of the contest over our political and historic rights between the Court and Patriot parties, from 1625 until the Patriots determined to secure their political rights by force of arms in 1776, — showing the ways by which the original historic wrong was supported and perpetuated under the crown.

CHAPTER I

UNDER CHARLES I., 1625-1641

HAVING considered the influence of contemporary politics on the published history, we have now to consider the political influences and circumstances which fostered that history for many generations.

Charles I. succeeded to the crown at his father's death, and, fortunately for our original charter rights, he was under personal obligations to both Sir Edwin Sandys and Mr. Nicholas Ferrar, Jr., who had been his most active friends, when, as Prince of Wales, his case against the Earl of Middlesex was before Parliament in 1624; and this circumstance may be regarded as one of the reasons why he, as king, was for many years more liberal in dealing with the political purposes of the political body of the colony than his father had been. He soon asked the old patriotic managers of the Virginia business to give him their opinion touching the best form of government, etc., for Virginia. In their reply they very astutely laid great stress on the past enmity of

the Earl of Middlesex to their old corporation;
claimed that it was chiefly through his instrumentality that their charters had been annulled,
and then asked his majesty to restore them.
This discourse for presentation to the king was
written very diplomatically. James I. was shielded
by laying blame for many things on Sir Thomas
Smith's party. The late managers, in regard to
their evidences, asserted in effect 'that the [royal]
commissioners had taken possession of the original
court books of the late company, and if they could
have gotten into their hands the copies of them
which Mr. Nicholas Ferrar had caused to be transcribed, they proposed doing the Patriot party in
that *corporation a wrong in their honors and
reputations by reforming and correcting the
said* originals so as to make them conform to
their [the royal] purposes; but before their
severe order for the copies came to Ferrar he had
delivered them to the Earl of Southampton, who
sent the [royal] commissioners word that he
would as soon part with the evidences of his land
as with the said copies; they being the evidences
of his honor in that service.' And the late
managers appealed earnestly to the committee of
the Privy Council then in charge of the colonies,
"*that howsoever your Lordships shall please
for the future to dispose of the companie, that
the records of their past actions may not be
corrupted and falsified.*" Their records had

been confiscated by the crown and their past actions had been falsified in the histories licensed under the crown; thus they were aware of the need for protection, and were evidently anxious to protect the truth of history so far as they possibly could. Previous to this earnest appeal to the crown, before he went to the Netherlands in the fall of 1624, the Earl of Southampton had sent the Danvers copies for safe keeping to his seat, Titchfield in Hampshire, and had given the Ferrar copies for safe keeping to Sir Robert Killigrew,[1] who had been appointed to the king's commission of July 25, 1624, but had been a member of the liberal party in the Virginia Corporation, and was in sympathy with the efforts to preserve the copies of their records. Charles I. replied to the discourse of the late managers of "the old Virginia Company" in a printed proclamation issued on May 23, 1625 — in a friendly way; but rejecting their appeal for a renewal of the corporation and body politic. He said "that our full resolution is that there maie be one uniform course of government in and through all our whole Monarchie. That the government of the Collonie of Virginia shall ymmediately depend uppon our Selfe, and not be commytted to anie Company, or Corporation, to whom it maie be proper to trust Matters of Trade and Commerce, but cannot be fitt or safe to communicate the

[1] See Packard's *Ferrar*, p. 156.

ordering of State Affaires be they of never soe meane consequence," etc.

The Ferrars had coöperated most earnestly with Sandys and other Patriots in their purpose to establish a popular course of government in this country. They had based great hopes on the popular charter rights of the corporation. They had been deprived of hope by James I.; the hope revived under Charles I. now vanished; like their friend, George Herbert the divine poet, they saw plainly that "the Court was made up of fraud, and titles, and flattery, and painted pleasures," and they determined to retire from the world of London. On June 9, 1625, Mrs. Mary Ferrar bought lands at Little Gidding, Huntingdonshire, in the names of her son Nicholas, and her nephew, Arthur Wodenoth, and the family soon after removed there; but we shall see that they never lost interest in Virginia.

When the death of Mr. John Pountis (who had been sent to prosecute their suit for our charter rights before James I. in 1624) became known in Virginia, "The Governor (Wyatt), Counsell, and Colony of Virginia assembled together," under the impression (real or pretended) that their former petition had not been presented to his majesty, determined to appeal to him again, and in June, 1625, sent their second petition for our charter rights to England by the hands of Sir George Yeardley. It was not then known in

Virginia that James I. was dead, and this petition was addressed to him. Yeardley arrived in England about two months after Charles I. had dissolved his first Parliament, changed the address, and presented to Charles I. the petition, which not only asked for many of our original charter rights, but also asked to have them confirmed by act of Parliament.

The second Parliament met in February, but was dissolved in June, 1626, and during the session, in March, Yeardley, a Patriot, was commissioned and sent back to Virginia as governor by Charles I., but " the Liberty of Generall Assemblyes" and other rights petitioned for were not yet restored.

Soon after, May 27, 1626, Sir Francis Wyatt, who as governor had continued to maintain the original popular form of government in the colony so far as possible since 1624, was sent from Virginia with a *third petition* from Virginians to the king and Privy Council for our original charter rights, etc. Finally, in the autumn of 1627, in response to repeated petitions, memorials, letters, and messengers from Virginia, and probably influenced thereto somewhat by the political contentions and conditions in England, Charles I. concluded to permit the colony to retain her General Assembly and other political charter rights, to which James I. was so bitterly opposed. The royal order restoring the House of Burgesses arrived in Virginia on March 4, 1628, and Captain Francis West, a Patriot who was then governor, immediately issued orders for the first election of burgesses under the crown, and summoned the General Assembly to meet at Jamestown on March 20, 1628.

Charles I. was constantly vacillating in this matter; having yielded to the appeals of the Patriots for a General Assembly in the autumn of 1627, on April 5, 1628, he commissioned John Harvey, a royalist, who had been at the head of the royal commission sent to Virginia by James I. in 1623, as governor of the colony. But grave political influences were at work. On May 18th, less than forty-five days after Harvey's appointment, the celebrated "Petition of Rights" was brought up in the third Parliament by our old friend, John Selden, and, after holding out as long as he could well do, on July 6th Charles I. found it advisable to assent to this petition, but prorogued the Parliament on the same day. The very first Parliament of Charles I. in 1625 had "opened the floodgates of a long contention with the crown," which was really a protection to the liberal political ideas while they were growing and gaining strength in America. And the breach between the king and the Commons was now (1628) really more complete than ever before. Charles I., realizing the fact that the colonists were becoming important factors in the politics of the realm, on September 22, 1628, sent an official letter to Governor Harvey, in which he yielded other charter rights to our body politic, renewing to the planters in Virginia their lands and privileges formerly granted, etc.

The corporation would doubtless have been glad to yield their past historic rights to the crown in order to aid in securing from the crown their political rights, and even while the contest over the political charter rights was going on in a way not entirely unfavorable to the Patriots, the royal ideas of their reform movement were being constantly impressed (without public protest) by the royal press on the mind of the public. A fourth edition of "Purchas his Pilgrimage" was published in 1626; Smith's "Generall Historie" was reissued in 1626, in 1627, and twice in 1632; his "True Travels," licensed in 1629, was published in 1630; and his "Advertisements for the Unexperienced Planters" was published in 1631. The views of these books were of course in accord with the views of the Court party, and opposed to the interests, acts, and political purposes of the Patriot party. The author of these books had become a subject of ridicule 'for writing so much and doing so little.' In August, 1625, Sir William Segar had a copy of a paper said to have been given to Smith by Sigismund Bathor recorded in the herald's office. Segar must have been imposed upon in this matter, as he was when he granted the royal arms of Aragon to Brandon, the common hangman of London, for the paper was evidently a forgery.[1]

In April, 1631, Sir John Harvey wrote from Virginia to Lord Dorchester that 'the self-will government, as formerlie hath bin practised in Virginia,' was still obtaining; and that the council contended that his — the royal governor's — " power extended noe further than a bare castinge voice," etc. The political ideas prevailing in Virginia were not without influence in England. In June, 1631, Charles I. appointed a large commission for advising him upon some course for establishing the advancement of the plantation of Virginia. This commission, being composed for the most part of members of the old Patriot party in the original body politic, favored the renewal of the ancient charters of the corporation [2] as the best course for the advancement of the colony, and in the autumn of 1631 they sent in a petition to Charles I. to that effect.

In reply to this petition the opposing Court party in England soon issued " Considerations

[1] See *Notes and Queries*, London, 7th series, vol. ix. pp. 1, 41, 102, 161, 223, and 281 ; and *The Genesis of the United States*, vol. ii. p. 1008.

[2] Charles I. had granted a similar charter to Massachusetts in March, 1629.

against the renewing of a Corporation for Virginia," in which they make use of some of their arguments of 1622–1624 : referring to the meetings of the old Virginia Courts (the old "seminary of sedition") as "mutinous meetings;" contending that the forms of government instituted in Ireland by James I. and in the West Indies by the kings of Spain were preferable to the popular course of our original body politic, which they asserted would "poyson that Plantation with factious spirits, and such as are refractory to Monarchicall government as all Corporations are — as is found by experience in the Corporation of New England." And they go on to justify the seizing of the company's papers and "Diaries" by James I. in 1624.

In August, 1631, the Earls of Dorset and Danby, Sir Robert Killigrew, Sir John Danvers, Sir Dudley Digges, Sir Francis Wyatt, Thomas Gibbes, George Sandys, Nicholas and John Ferrar, Gabriel Barber, and others of the commission, sent letters to Virginia in the interest of the proposed renewal of the charter; and in furtherance of that object the council in Virginia in December, 1631, buried their opposition to, came to an accord with, and entered into an agreement of peace and reconciliation with, the royal governor, Harvey. About the same time the planters in Virginia sent in their petitions for the renewal of the charter. These petitions from Virginia reached England early in 1632. In March, the adventurers in England held a meeting, and " expressed a grateful readiness to accept his Majesties grace and bounty in proffering a new charter of Restitution of a Company, with confirmation of all their ancient Territorie, rights and privileges whatsoever, — some points of government only, with some few other reservations, excepted."

But in June, 1632, Charles I., constantly vacillating, granted Maryland within the bounds of " their ancient Territories " to Lord Baltimore, regardless of the protest of Virginians. And it was about this time that, at the instance of Lord Baltimore, the judgment of the King's Bench in the *quo warranto* case (June, 1624) against their charter was entered upon record for the first time.

Sir Robert Killigrew died in May, 1633, and, in the continued effort to preserve the copies of the records, left the Ferrar copies to the care of Edward Sackville Earl of Dorset, who had also been a member of the Patriot party in the Virginia Company, and was then at the head of the Liberal Colonial Commission appointed by Charles I. in June, 1631.

In the summer of 1633 this commission held meetings and consultations with divers of the chief planters of Virginia (who had evidently come to England for that purpose), at which it was resolved to urge the king to a compliance with their petition[1] praying for a renewal of their ancient charter. Charles I. had visited the Ferrars at their home, "Little Gidding," in May, 1633, and seems now to have been disposed to grant their request for a renewal of their ancient charter, with certain alterations; but was not willing to yield to them Lord Baltimore's patent. And the Virginians were not willing to yield to the crown their ancient boundary rights, and therefore their request was finally denied them.

The king then revoked the liberal commission of 1631, and on May 8, 1834, appointed a "commission for governing the colonies" of an entirely different complexion, composed almost entirely of opponents of the popular course of government: William Laud Archbishop of Canterbury, Thomas Lord Coventry (the old advocate of the Court party in the *quo warranto* suit of 1624), Richard Neyle Archbishop of York, and nine high officers of state, several of whom had aided James I. in his contest against our charter rights in 1620–1624; and under this commission the grant to Lord Baltimore, which had been opposed by the former commission, was confirmed. All the boroughs or corporations of Virginia had been entitled, since 1619,

[1] Sent from Virginia in March, received by the king in May, and considered by the Privy Council in May, June, July, and August, 1633.

to representation in the House of Burgesses, but under the new commission for governing the colonies, Virginia was divided in 1634 into "eight shires," and representation restricted to them. In order to prevent alarm among Virginians over these and other infringements of their charter rights by the royal commission, the colonial committee of the Privy Council on August 1, 1634, wrote to Governor Harvey in Virginia that "in the present proceeding it is not intended that interests which men (planters) have settled when you were a corporation should be impeached; that for the present the planters may enjoy their estates with the same freedom and privileges as they did before the recalling of their patents." The comfort in this letter was not definite, and must have seemed very cold to the old Patriots in Virginia.

Under the royal rule of the royal commission in England, and of Sir John Harvey the royal governor in Virginia, the spirit of freedom which had always inspired the planters was soon aroused into what the Court party regarded as a rebellion. The revolt was led by John West, William Claiborne, Samuel Matthews, John Utie, William Pierce, William Ferrar, William Perry, George Menefie, Thomas Harwood, Dr. John Pott, Nicholas Marlier or Martian (an ancestor of George Washington), and other old members of the original of the body politic of this nation, and in May, 1635, resulted in the removal of Sir John Harvey, a royalist, and the election by the General Assembly of Captain John West, a Patriot, as governor in Harvey's place. Harvey went to England, arrived at Plymouth soon after the New England charter of 1620 had been surrendered to the king, gave the king his account of the Virginia affair, was reappointed and sent back to Virginia, where he arrived early in 1637. In the spring of that year John West (governor by election of the representatives of the people, 1635-1637), Samuel Matthews, John Utie, and others " were sent prisoners to England to answer some objections in the Star Chamber," and Sergeant-Major George Donne [1] was sent at the same time by Governor Harvey as his agent, " to prosecute those persons that were lately seditious in Virginia." While in England, Donne (who went to Virginia with Harvey in 1630) wrote a very long " review of Virginia " to Charles I., which is a discourse from the point of view of the Court party, rather than a review. He was opposed to the popular course of government which obtained in Virginia — " where no acknowledgement of A Superior is," and " such presumptuousness in men of turbulent and unquiett spirits as have, I am confident, from the first footinge in Virginia to this pre-

[1] A son of Rev. John Donne (1573-1631), the eminent divine and poet.

sent, much hindered the progress thereof. How this Assertion findes warrant is evident by the late action of some particulers fiery and headstrong in their disorder and conspiracy against your Majesties Commissioned Governor Harvey, at this present in that Country." He said that the conspiracy against the royal governor was "noe doubt long in plotting though lately practised," and urged the king to put a stop to the popular course of government in the colony, which he describes as "by A multitude whose Pollicy is gayne, whose gravitye is giddinesse, whose Discretion is noyse and tumult," encouraging mutinies and rebellions against the royal government.

But the ears of Charles I. were not yet entirely closed to the popular side; the liberal party in Virginia still had friends near his person or in correspondence with him, and among these may be mentioned Sir John Danvers and Mr. George Sandys (brother of Sir Edwin Sandys, who had died in 1629), who were then gentlemen of the king's Privy Chamber. He was also on very friendly terms with the fourth Earl of Southampton, John Ferrar, and others; and on January 21, 1639, he appointed Sir Francis Wyatt, the Patriot, to succeed Harvey, the Royalist, as governor of Virginia. Wyatt arrived in the colony in November, 1639, and at once ordered an election of burgesses, who met in the General Assembly of January, 1640, at which time it was determined to make another effort to secure the original charter rights of the body politic of the colony. George Sandys was appointed as the agent of the colony in England; petitions for their ancient charter rights were prepared and sent over to him. The fourth Parliament of Charles I. met in April, 1640, but the king never could get along with his Parliaments, and he dissolved it within a month. His fifth and last Parliament, which was destined to "dissolve" the king, met on November 13, 1640. The petitions from Virginia probably reached England in the autumn of 1640, after both Sandys and Danvers had retired from the king's personal service. The open contest between the crown and the Commons was in sight. The Patriots in England "had been led a race" by Charles I.: they now determined to look to the Parliament; and George Sandys presented these petitions for restoring the company's charters, not to Charles I., but, in "the name of the Adventurers and Planters in Virginia," to the House of Commons in the beginning of the Long Parliament, and under the auspices of the popular party in that Parliament "the Virginia patent was taken out again under the broad Seal of England."

CHAPTER II

CIVIL WAR, 1641-1646

THE long controversy between the crown and the House of Commons became an open contest on the execution of Thomas Wentworth Earl of Strafford, in May, 1641.

In response to the petition of Governor Wyatt, the General Assembly, and patriotic planters of Virginia, the Virginia charter had been renewed by Parliament: Charles I. naturally felt that he would need a stronger hand in the colony than Wyatt if Virginia was to be kept loyal to the crown; and in August, 1641, he commissioned Sir William Berkeley (a strong Royalist) to supersede Wyatt, the Patriot, as governor. He arrived in Virginia in February, 1642, and at once began to take steps for holding the colony loyal to the crown. To offset the regranting of the ancient charter by Parliament in reply to the petition of the General Assembly under Wyatt, he promptly called another assembly to meet under his own auspices — which issued a strong declaration,[1] written from the point of view of the

[1] In "the Declaration against the Company," as printed in Hening's *Statutes at Large of Virginia*, vol. i. p. 231, the reference to "depositions taken at a Grand Assembly anno 1632" is really to depositions taken by Harvey when he was a commissioner or agent of James I. in Virginia in 1623 (o. s.). It is an error of the typesetter.

Royalist or Court party, against the renewal of the charters, assuring the king that George Sandys, in presenting the former petition to the House of Commons, "had mistook his instructions." The paper is of especial value, because it shows the line of argument used by the Royalists against the charter rights to the people as a political body. This Declaration of Berkeley's Assembly was sent in April, 1642, directly to Charles I. himself, who replied in July following to the effect that he had no idea of surrendering "his colony to any company." Thus the petitions from both parties in Virginia prevailed with their respective parties in England. The Parliament was soon in the ascendant, and it came to pass that the colonists virtually enjoyed their "ancient charter rights" until 1660. The king had rejected the propositions of peace from Parliament on June 12th; in August following he set up his standard in Nottingham, and the civil war began in earnest.

Parliament, having set up a rival government in England, on December 4, 1643, appointed a rival commission for governing the plantations in America, with Philip Herbert Earl of Pembroke and Edward Montague Earl of Manchester at the head of it; and among its members were John Pym and Oliver Cromwell.

Parliament, having an issue of its own with the crown, had been from the first disposed to lend a hand to the popular party in the Virginia Corporation in all their past controversies with the Court party; but, under the Sandys-Ferrar influence, Charles I. had not been entirely unfriendly to the reform government which had been instituted in our country, and I doubt if there was any desire for a separation from the crown of Great Britain. Certainly there was no wisdom in such desire until the colonies became strong enough, when united in a corporate capacity, to defend themselves and to maintain their own rights. Although the opposition to the absolute tyranny then exercised by the crown in England had led up to the Commonwealth, and had furnished the inspiration which had enabled the managers of the business to establish the colonies regardless of all difficulties, the colonists did not wish to be "slaves to the Parliament in England" any more than they did to the king. In fact their purpose had been to be attached to the crown of England, "to have one common king with the mother country," but a parliament of their own, and to have no laws, taxes, etc., put upon them, save by their own consent, as enacted in their own parliament, or General Assembly. Hence it may be doubted if Sir William Berkeley's task in preventing open rebellion against the crown in Virginia was a very difficult one. Especially as, although the colony was under a governor appointed by the crown, the people were left very much on their own resources, and almost independent of the government in England, whether Cavalier or Roundhead, from 1642 to 1652.

CHAPTER III

PARLIAMENT, ETC., 1646-1660[1]

PARLIAMENT had been kept so busy in England that, although it had reissued the original charter to the body politic of the colony, near the beginning of the session, little or nothing was done in the matter of settling the government of Virginia under the Commonwealth, until September, 1651, when Robert Dennis, Richard Bennett, Thomas Stagg, and William Claiborne were appointed commissioners of Parliament and sent with a fleet to Virginia. After arriving in Virginia, the surviving commissioners and the Grand Assembly of Virginia soon entered into an agreement, signed on March 22, 1652 (N. S.), in which the Commonwealth of England granted to the colony of Virginia her former liberties, privileges, and an-

---

[1] Charles I. fled to Scotland in May, 1646; was given up by the Scots to Parliament in September following, and was executed February 9, 1649 (N. S.). The Commonwealth of England was established on the death of Charles I., but the first charter thereof was not drawn up by the council of officers until December, 1653. England was under the government of the Parliament, or "A Democracie," 1646-1653; the Protectorate of Oliver Cromwell, December, 1653,-September, 1658, and of Richard Cromwell, 1658-April, 1659; and the Civil War resumed, 1659-1660.

cient limits; free trade, exemption from taxation save by her own Assembly, etc., — that is to say, the charter rights of the original corporation of the colony.

From March, 1652, to 1660 the colony was virtually ruled by the House of Burgesses, — "the representatives of the people." Richard Bennett, a Patriot, was elected by that House on May 10, 1652, to serve as governor for three years; Edward Digges, a Patriot, was elected in 1665, and Samuel Matthews, a Patriot, in 1658. He died in January, 1660, before the expiration of his term. Civil war was renewed in England in 1659; but the restoration of Charles II. was soon in sight, and the General Assembly of Virginia elected Sir William Berkeley, a Royalist, as governor, in March, 1660.

The Commonwealth had fulfilled its mission, and Providence had aided in fostering the spirit which animated the founders of this nation until their projected political purposes had taken an ineradicable hold in Virginia.

CHAPTER IV

OF THE CONTROL OVER HISTORIC RECORDS

If we consider the character of the controversies between the Court and Patriot parties, it will be seen that it was not possible to correct the historic wrong committed by James I. so long as the evidences and the press continued under the control of the crown.

In the reign of Elizabeth the Star Chamber Court granted a decree prohibiting the printing of books without the license of one of the archbishops or of the bishop of London, or their representatives. In February, 1629, certain printers presented a petition to Parliament, complaining that Laud's chaplain had refused to license certain books. John Selden, in presenting this petition of the printers, said: "There is no law to prevent the printing of any book in England, but only a decree in the Star Chamber. Therefore, that a man should be fined, imprisoned, and his goods taken from him, is a great invasion of the liberty of the subject." But the correction of this wrong was not accomplished at that time. "Printers and authors continued to be brought before the High Commission, and taught to obey the restrictions imposed upon them at the risk of fine and imprisonment."[1]

I will note some examples bearing on our premises. When Mr. Nicholas Ferrar, Jr., sent George Herbert's poem, "The Church Militant," to Cambridge, in 1633, to be licensed for the press, the vice-chancellor would by no means allow the printing of the noted verses: —

"Religion stands a-tiptoe in our land,
Ready to pass to the American strand,

[1] Gardiner's *History of England*, vii. p. 130.

> When height of malice and prodigious lusts,
> Impudent sinning, witchcrafts, and distrusts,
>   .   .   .   .   .   .
> Then shall religion to America flee."

And Mr. Ferrar would by no means allow the book to be printed without them, and he finally had his way.

In April, 1637, John Lilburne was condemned in the Star Chamber to be whipped, pilloried, and imprisoned for publishing seditious pamphlets. While in the pillory he spoke to the people against the tyranny of the Court party, and scattered pamphlets from his pockets. During life he continued fighting for the cause of freedom, and was upheld by the voice of the people. Thomas Jefferson's grandmother, Jane Rogers, of Shadwell Street, London, was certainly related to "Wm. Lilburne Esqre of Kenton in the Bishoprick of Durham," of the same family, and Jefferson may have descended from John's brother, General Robert Lilburne, the regicide.

It has been said that 'the mere assembling of the Long Parliament on Nov. 13, 1640, took the gag entirely off the press;' but this is not strictly correct. The courts of Star Chamber and High Commission, which had been condemned by the Patriots in various Parliaments since 1607 as grievances, were abolished by the Long Parliament in July, 1641, and the press was relieved of their oppression; but the press was not yet free. John Milton was the foremost champion in that age for the liberty of unlicensed printing; but even he asserted in his "Areopagitica" (published in 1644), 'that it is of greatest concernment in the church and Commonwealth, to have a vigilant eye how Books demean themselves, as well as Men; and thereafter to confine, imprison, and do sharpest justice to them as malefactors; for Books are not absolutely dead things, but do contain a potencie of life in them to be as active as that soul was whose progeny they are; nay, they do preserve as in a viol the purest efficacy and extraction of that living intellect that bred them; they are as lively, and as vigorously productive as those fabulous Dragon's teeth; and, being sown up and down, may chance to spring up armed men.'

There was very little if any printing done after 1622 by members of the Patriot party relative to Virginia until the press was free from the control of the crown. Under the Commonwealth John Ferrar, the surviving deputy, and other old Patriots in England, corresponded with many old planters in Virginia, and aided in publishing several books about the colony, among these being Wodenoth's "Short Collection;" "The Discovery of New Britaine," by Edward Bland and others, dedicated to Sir John Danvers; "Virginia and Maryland," and other tracts of less political importance to our earliest history.

Of these Wodenoth's tract was of the greatest political and historical importance. During the civil war, about the year 1644, at which time he was the deputy governor of the Bermudas Islands Company, Mr. Arthur Wodenoth, who had been a member of the liberal party in the Virginia Corporation, a first cousin to the Ferrar brothers, wrote "An account and observation taken by A. W., a true friend and servant to Sir John Danvers, and the Parliament interest, containing a great part of his [Danvers'] more public transactions concerning the plantation of Virginia," etc. Mr. Wodenoth, who is well known as the friend and executor of George Herbert, the divine poet, died soon after writing the book, leaving the manuscript to his cousin, Will Wodenoth, with instructions to publish it at a seasonable time. Before this time came Will Wodenoth had died. The book was finally published in 1651 under the title of "A Short Collection of the most remarkable passages from the original to the dissolution of the Virginia Company," 1609–1624. Having evidently been written largely from memory after a considerable lapse of time, Arthur Wodenoth was not sure of dates, but asked his cousin to "view the court books of the Virginia Company and the orders of the Privy Council Board, and [before publication] to add therefrom the year of our Lord in the Margent at every main transaction;" but these books and orders were not available, and the tract had to be published, as written, *without a single date.* For this reason it is not always clear, if taken by itself; but after adding the dates in the " Margent " and considering it in connection with the orders and other records now available it becomes of great historic value. With the light shed upon it by other evidences, and with the light which it sheds upon other evidences, we are enabled to see many of the political purposes inspiring our original body politic which were obscured or obliterated from the history as licensed by the crown. Nothing relative to the political character of the movement could have been published by any one during the reigns of James I. or Charles I. Nothing of the sort was ever published by Sir Edwin Sandys or any of the leading patriotic statesmen among the managers of the business. This book, published at the first seasonable time, was the first publication, which may be called contemporary, written boldly from the political point of view of the Patriot party; and although it was not written by one of the leading statesmen who had managed the political features of the movement, the author was a man of established character, of means and of personal influence, intimate with the Ferrars and Sir John Danvers, and evidently knew much relative to those features; and the Court party knew this, for his book was manifestly suppressed after the restoration of the king in 1660.[1]

About 1655 John Ferrar wrote the memoirs of his brother Nicholas (who had died in 1637); he may have intended publishing it — if so the publication was prevented by John's own death in the autumn of 1657. After 1660 the memoirs would not have passed the censors of the press, and they were not printed until 1790, and were not made use of by our historians until after that time. Of the leading managers in England, John Ferrar, Sr., was probably the last survivor. Henry Earl of Southampton died in 1624; Sir Thomas Smythe in 1625; Robert Johnson and William Canning about 1628; William Lord Cavendish in 1628; Sir Edwin Sandys in 1629; Nicholas Ferrar, Jr., in 1637; Sir John Danvers in 1655, and John Ferrar, Sr., in 1657. Of the leading managers in Virginia, De La Warr, Dale, and many others died before the crown began the open attempt to annul our charter rights. Gates, Yeardley, Francis West, and many others died before John Ferrar. John West, Samuel Matthews, Richard Bennet, William Claiborne, and other old planters lived as long as or longer than Ferrar. These old members of our original body politic were able to nourish and to protect

---

[1] I made use of it in compiling *The First Republic in America*. I cannot find that it was ever used before as evidence by any one in writing history.

the tree of Liberty as it was growing from the seed which they had aided in depositing in our sacred soil until it was strong enough to resist the coming storms; and to inspire their posterity with the determination to "protect that tree" with the same vital force which had inspired them to plant that seed.

Although naturally more anxious to protect their charter rights than their history, the old Patriots, who had a personal interest in preserving the true history of the colonial movement of 1606–1624, probably did whatever they could do toward preserving evidences; but whatever they did had to be done privately — they were never able to publish anything in Virginia, for *all* had "passed over the river" before any printing press was allowed in Virginia.

I should have noted before this, but I suppose that it has been well understood, that the suppression of the truth in this matter was not confined to England, but also obtained in Virginia so long as the colony was under the crown. Many of the evidences of our original body politic were sent to the colony — during 1609–1624 for service and after 1624 for preservation; but they were not secure even in Virginia from the Court party, for the royal control over evidences prevailed in the colony after it was resumed by the crown. John Harvey, who served at the head of the royal commission of 1623–

1625 sent to Virginia by James I. for the purpose of procuring evidence to justify him in annulling the company's charters, was one of the earliest regular royal governors. Another was Sir William Berkeley, who in 1671 thanked God that there were no free schools nor printing in Virginia, and hoped there would not be for an hundred years — "for learning had brought disobedience [to kings] and heresy and sects into the world, and *printing had divulged them,* and libels against the best government [the king's]. God keep us from both!" Such governors were as well calculated to obliterate evidences favorable to liberal ideas as they were to destroy the popular plant growing from the seed which had been deposited in Virginia, and the crown, we may rest assured, expected them to do *both.*

CHAPTER V

NOTES ON THE WAY FROM 1660 TO 1746

It is not necessary to continue the outline, in any detail, of the controversy we are treating of; but it will be well to note "a sign" along the route now and then to guide the student on his way.

After the restoration of Charles II. in 1660 the iron hand of royal authority was placed most firmly on the press, and among the first books burnt by royal proclamation were the works of Milton in defense of the rights of the people.

The first biographical sketch of the author of our earliest history was compiled during the civil war by Rev. Thomas Fuller, chaplain to Ralph Hopton, to whom, with others, Charles II. in 1649 granted the Northern Neck of Virginia. Fuller died in August, 1661, but the publication of his "Worthies" was completed by his son in 1662, and dedicated to Charles II. Fuller had no personal knowledge of the facts, and his views of Smith's services in Virginia as a representative of James I. were those of the Court party, to which he belonged; but he knew personally something of Smith's life in England, and his sketch is important, because it throws light on the contemporary opinions, even of members of the Court party, regarding the personal matter in his publications, and on the personal character and position in society of a man whom James I. nominated to be of his council in Virginia, and whom the crown licensed to publish the history of this great reform movement.

In considering the effect of politics on our history, we must consider both the House of Commons in England and the House of Burgesses in Virginia. The convention Parliament which restored Charles II. in May, 1660, was not in full political accord with the king, and was dissolved by him in December following. The new

Parliament, which met in May, 1661, was more in accord with the crown; but contentions began again, and the king finally dissolved it in December, 1678. A second Parliament met in March, 1679, but party spirit ran very high, and it was dissolved within four months. The third met in October, 1680, and was dissolved in three months, etc. The same weapons — of proroguing, adjourning, and finally dissolving — came to be used by the royal governors of the colony in their contentions with our House of Burgesses. It must be noted that Charles II. held on to one Parliament from 1661 to 1678, and Berkeley held on to one House of Burgesses from 1661 to 1676.

The first House of Burgesses elected after the restoration, which met April 1, 1661, was apparently very loyal to Charles II. The charter to the Virginia Corporation had been restored by act of Parliament about twenty years before, and Virginians had been governing themselves under that charter since 1652; the majority of "the Company" were now planters, and the members of this House of Burgesses were really members of that body politic; but they evidently felt the need of conciliating the king. Charles Campbell, on page 252 of his history of the colony, says that Governor Berkeley was dispatched to England in 1661 to oppose "the navigation act." From the act of assembly as published,[1] he seems

[1] See Hening's *Statutes at Large of Virginia*, vol. ii. p. 17.

to have been sent to oppose the oppression of some company; but the name of the company is not given, and several other words in the manuscript were not legible. The evidence in the premises was under the control of the crown, and what remains is not sufficient to enable any one to know the facts. It is probable, however, that the Burgesses feared that Charles II. would now carry out the former plans of James I.; for there is sufficient evidence to prove that the colonists still wished to retain their original charter rights, and that there was reason for this fear is manifest.

In May, 1669, Charles II. issued a second patent confirming the grant of September, 1649 (given when he was in exile), of the Northern Neck of Virginia lying north of the northern boundary as conveyed to a company by the charter of 1606; and this was the beginning of a long controversy, between the crown and the body politic of the colony, over boundary rights.

In 1673 Charles II. granted "A demise" of the "entire territory" of the colony of Virginia to the Earl of Arlington and Lord Culpeper for thirty-one years. This, of course, was at once opposed by Virginians. In September, 1674, Colonel Francis Morryson, Secretary Thomas Ludwell, and Major-General Robert Smith were appointed "Agents for the Governor, Council, and Burgesses of the Country of Virginia and

Territory of Accomak," and sent to England with a petition to procure a revocation of that "demise," and, also, with a petition to obtain from the crown a confirmation of the ancient charter rights, liberties, privileges, and properties of the colony. They opened negotiations with the crown for these rights in June, 1675. These agents were really asking for the same political and property rights which had been the platform of the Patriot party since 1609; which party never acknowledged that our charter rights had ever been legally annulled; but there was always need for diplomacy in wording such petitions to the crown, and these agents yielded the point, acknowledged that James I. had annulled the original charter, and then based their petition on the ground that "although for the misgovernment of the Company the charter was demanded in a *Quo Warranto,* yet did the said king forthwith promise and declare that a charter should be renewed, with the former privileges, to the planters." And among other things they assert, almost in the original words of Sir Edwin Sandys, as a charter right that "Virginians should not be taxed without their own consent."[1]

---

[1] While these negotiations were going on in England, Sir William Berkeley's acts in Virginia were turning Bacon's war against the Indians into what the Court party called "Bacon's Rebellion."

In reply to their petition, after many difficulties, and two years' delay, the Virginians gained nothing from Charles II., save a charter (signed October 20, 1676) which, instead of confirming their original charter rights, was "little more than a declaration of the dependence of the colony on the crown of England." And the inhabitants of Virginia were destined to receive very much the same sort of treatment in reply to their appeals and petitions for an hundred years longer.

It has been said: "In other countries it has been thought hard enough to have the printing press clogged by the interference of official licensers and spies; in Virginia the printing press was forbidden to work at all." The crown, persisting in the purpose of obliterating the liberal ideas which had given vitality to the colony, had never permitted a printing press to be set up in Virginia. Yet, in some way, a press was finally introduced about 1680, for printing the laws of the representative of the people — the House of Burgesses. But early in 1683 the royal governor, Thomas Lord Culpeper, called John Buckner (the owner) and the printer before him, and ordered them not to print anything thereafter until his majesty's pleasure should be known. The next year, when Francis Lord Howard, of Effingham, arrived in Virginia as governor, he brought orders " *to allow no per-*

son to use a printing press in Virginia on any occasion whatsoever."

The restoration of Charles II. had not obliterated the desire for "a more free government," either in Virginia or in England, and we find the old ideas of national rights and liberties inspiring the revolution which removed James II., and placed William and Mary on the throne of Great Britain in February, 1689.

It is generally stated that "the press of Great Britain has been free since 1693;" but the freedom of the press continued to be subject to many restrictions, some of the laws of libel and of loyalty — to church and state — being especially severe. And no person was yet allowed to use a printing press in Virginia on any occasion whatsoever.

In 1705 Robert Beverley published in London the first history written by a Virginian, covering the period 1606–1624. When Beverley was compiling this history he does not seem to have had the use of one particle of the evidence of our original body politic, — not a single one of the numerous publications of the managers and not a scrap of their record. More than a third of his narrative relates to the formative period of 1606–1624, and the whole of this is based on the histories licensed under James I. The ideas expressed by him of this movement are the ideas which he had derived from those histories.

In 1738 Sir William Keith published a history of Virginia, in which about 20,000 words relate to the three years (1607–1610), while the colony was under the crown, and only about 6000 words to the fifteen years (1610–1625), while the colony was under the new charter. Like Beverley, he had none of the records of the Virginia Company; none of the publications of the managers of the business; but relied entirely on Beverley and the histories licensed by the crown. His " history " and Beverley's have an especial value as guides, because they show how completely the purpose of James I. to obliterate the true idea of our origin as a nation had been carried out under royal rule up to that time, and what our ideas of this movement would now be, if no other evidences at all had been preserved save those given to the public under the auspices of the crown.

As a further illustration of how completely the records were suppressed in the public repositories at this time, it may be mentioned that although three editions of the great work, "Rymer's Fœdera," were published between 1704 and 1745, neither of the three American charters (1606, 1609, and 1612) are given in either edition; the first important document given bearing on the movement being the royal commission of May 19, 1623, appointed to aid James I. in annulling our charter rights, and the next the commission of July 25, 1624, appointed after the charters had been overthrown in the King's Bench, to aid the king in confiscating the company's evidences and annulling their historic rights. Thus it would seem that at this time the purpose of the crown to obliterate from the pages of history the truth regarding our origin as a nation had been accomplished. But many copies of the evidences of our original corporation were then being privately preserved in Virginia, and although not available to the historian, many other evidences were then being providentially preserved in England, and thenceforward these evidences were to be brought to light from time to time by the laborer in the field of original research in search of the truth.

CHAPTER VI

STITH'S "HISTORY OF VIRGINIA," 1747

The press finally circumvented (so to speak) the opposition of the crown by worming its way into Virginia via Maryland. As early as 1727 William Parks had established a printing press at Annapolis, where he printed for the governments of Maryland and Virginia. He set up a printing press in Williamsburg, probably in 1729, and finally removed to that city to reside in 1736. He was the first legally employed printer in Virginia. "Stith's History of Virginia," which issued from his press in 1747, was the first historical book published in Virginia, and it related entirely to the formative period of 1606–1624.

The Rev. William Stith was far better equipped with evidences on which to base his history than any previous Virginia historian had ever been; but owing to the long-continued purpose of the crown to obliterate the truth, he was very far from being fully equipped, even if he had taken the proper political view, and even if the press of the colony had not still been virtually under the control of the royal government. It is very remarkable that in compiling his history, although he evidently had access to the leading libraries in Virginia, he did not have the use of a single one of the contemporary prints published by the managers of the movement, the history of which he proposed to write, and it was not possible for him to understand the case properly without them. His chief published authorities were the histories of Smith and Purchas, which had previously been for so long the only authorities available to historians. He had none of the national official records in the premises; of Spain, France, or the Netherlands, and but few of those of England, and he could not have understood the movement correctly without them. But some of the corporation records — or rather copies of them, the originals having been confiscated by the crown in 1624 — were now being brought to light, and he had a good many of these relative to events after 1618; but only a few of the records prior to that date, and it was not possible for him to write his history completely without them. He knew that several documents issued by the Virginia courts had been sent over by Sir George Yeardley, but he had the use of only one of them; and seems to have been under the mistaken idea that the "great charter" and the commission of 1618 for establishing the General Assembly in Virginia had not been issued until after the changes in the presiding officials of the corporation in 1619. He had, however, in manuscript complete copies of the following really important documents: —

The Royal Charter of April 20, 1606.

The King's Instructions of Nov. 30, 1606.

The Orders of the King's Council, Dec. 20, 1606.

The Advice of the King's Council, Dec. 20, 1606.

The King's Ordinance and Constitution, March 19, 1607.

The First Charter to the Body Politic, June 2, 1609.

The Second Charter to the Body Politic, March 22, 1612.

The Instructions of the Virginia Court to Yeardley, November, 1618.

The Instructions of the Virginia Court to Wyatt, August, 1621.

The Ordinance and Constitution of the Body Politic, 1621.

The copies which had been preserved in Virginia of the papers sent to England from the General Assembly of March, 1624, by Pountis in 1624, namely: —

A. Their Answer to Johnson's Declaration.

B. Their Answer to Butler's Unmasking.

C. Their Petition to James I.

D. Their Letter to the Privy Council; enclosing —

E. The Declaration of the Ancient Planters.

F. Their Answer to Harvey's Propositions; and —

G. The Laws, Orders, etc., passed by them during the session of February and March, 1624.[1]

" And last, but not least," —

The copies of the Acts of the General Courts of the Company (" The Seminary of Sedition ") in London, from the Quarter Court of May 8, 1619, to that of June 17, 1624.

Next to the charters of 1609 and 1612, the copies of the records of the Virginia courts were the most important documents used by

[1] See *The First Republic in America*, pp. 571–582.

Stith. They covered the period from May, 1619, to June, 1624, but contain many references to prior dates, and Stith's history of events from 1618 to 1624 is largely based on them. As Stith did not have a proper understanding of the case, he misunderstood these records in several particulars. The popular form of government had been instituted in Virginia during the administration of Sir Thomas Smith. The parties in the company during the period covered by these records had originated in disputes over business matters, and not over political rights; but it came to pass that Sir Thomas Smith's party, in order to accomplish their business objects, catering to the national Court party, were finally willing to surrender their popular charter rights to the crown. As William Canning expressed it, "to give in their Charter and not to contest with the King about the government," as he thought such a contest must end in their defeat. The party led by Sir Edwin Sandys, which controlled the Virginia courts during the period of these records, was not willing to give up their charter nor to yield "their liberty of governing themselves" to the crown. The political contest was really between the Court party, the advocates of an imperial form of government — the king's side, and the Patriot party, the advocates of " a more free form of government — the people's side ; "

but it would have been folly for the Sandys party to make the issue directly with the Court party. They could only hope to succeed by using discretion in all ways, and their policy was, as these records show, to attack the party in their corporation which was willing to yield to the purposes of James I., rather than the Court party, or crown itself. Hence these records, unless the conditions then obtaining are properly taken into consideration, produce the impression that the political contest was between the parties in the corporation led respectively by Sir Thomas Smith and Sir Edwin Sandys. Mr. Stith was evidently under this mistaken impression, for in his history, on page 330, he says: ' Although Captain John Smith was certainly no friend to the Company, yet his History is much in Honour and Vindication of Sir Thomas Smith and his government.' The history licensed by the crown was in vindication of the king's (James I.) government (not Sir Thomas Smith's), and therefore it is in accord with Sir Thomas Smith's party when that party is in accord with the Court party; but it is really in opposition to the management and political purposes of the body politic from the beginning, and it is as unjust to the administration of Sir Thomas Smith as to that of Sandys and Southampton. And for the aforesaid reason these records have sometimes been considered as evidences against the

Sir Thomas Smith administration, and therefore as indorsements of the history licensed by the crown for the period prior to 1618, rather than as evidences in defense of our original political charter rights and against the purposes of the Court party itself.

Mr. Stith praised " the Virginia Company," yet he regarded the annulling of the " Company's Charters " as " an event certainly of Benefit and Advantage to the Country, as we in America find by Experience, that it is better to be under a Royal government, than in the Hands of Proprietors, in what shape or Manner soever." I believe myself that everything may have happened for the best, and fallen on its due time; but " the Colony in Virginia " never belonged, in the sense which Stith seems to have supposed, to " the Company in London." Under the system projected under the charters of 1609 and 1612, the proprietors of the Colony in Virginia were members of a corporation and body politic composed of adventurers and planters; and even when Mr. Stith was writing this opinion the vital principles of that body were still shaping our destiny, and were soon after inspiring the minds of many of our patriotic people to a conviction that the time was near at hand when it would be of " Benefit and Advantage to the Country " to have the government in " the hands of the proprietors " of the country. This purpose was finally consummated, and "we in America find by experience" that it is certainly of "Benefit and Advantage to the Country."

On pages 36 to 42 of his history, Stith criticised adversely and placed a very correct estimate on the form of government designed for the plantations in America by James I. in 1606–1607; but not taking into consideration the political conditions then obtaining he failed to appreciate the disastrous effect of royal politics on the histories published under the auspices of the crown, and after thus condemning the design of James I. he goes on to base his history of the next ten years on the contemporary histories published in vindication of that very form of government. Then when the censored story meets the portion of the corporation's records which he had in hand he goes back to his first view-point again, rejects the royal views, and bases his history on these records for the last seven years of the period. Then he takes the other view again, and contends that the charters ought to have been annulled, and finally claims that they had never been legally annulled. He changed his political view-point with the evidence which he happened to be using; hence he was sometimes on the side of the Patriot party, then on the side of the Court party, and sometimes "at sea."

He paid no attention to the political conditions

controlling the case in 1606–1624, and it was not possible for him to write a correct account without doing so. Although he impeached the history licensed by the crown " at both ends," so to speak, he relied upon the history, which he had impeached, for his account of events during 1607–1617, the period in which it was peculiarly to the political purpose of James I., who controlled the press, and to the personal interest of his licensed agent, the historian who wrote the book, to convey false ideas of the movement. The political point of view, not only of 1606–1610, and 1610–1617, but of the whole period, 1606–1624, was overlooked by Stith, and has been misunderstood, or not considered, by the subsequent historians who have followed him.

Since 1747 the history licensed by the crown has continued to be generally relied on for the earlier period, 1606–1617; but Stith, rather than Smith, has been followed as the historian of the later period, 1618–1624. Although Mr. Stith was a minister under the crown, and did not always take the patriotic point of view, his history presented to the public for the first time the charters to our original body politic, together with extended extracts from so much of the record of that body as to cause our people to become more and more familiar with their original charter rights; and although so much of our earliest history was still obscured, those rights became more and more sacred to them.

CHAPTER VII

AN ACCOUNT OF THE ORIGINAL COPIES WHICH HAVE BEEN PRESERVED OF THE VIRGINIA COURT RECORDS FROM MAY, 1619, TO JUNE, 1624

I now think that the copies used by Stith were evidently the Danvers copies which had been sent by Southampton to Titchfield in 1624, and not a portion of the Ferrar 'copies of *all* the court books, and all other writings belonging to the company,' which Southampton gave to Sir Robert Killigrew for safe keeping, as I thought when I wrote "The First Republic in America."[1]

These two volumes were taken to Titchfield for preservation in the autumn of 1624. Henry Wriothesley, third Earl of Southampton and last treasurer of the Virginia Company, died soon after. His son Thomas, the fourth earl, inherited the volumes. As was the case with Sir Edwin and George Sandys, John and Nicholas Ferrar, and Sir John Danvers, the fourth Earl of Southampton became a close friend to Charles I. It is interesting to note in this connection, first, that the last time Charles I. came to Little Gidding he came for protection, 'very privately, and in the night of May 12, 1646. Mr. Nicholas Ferrar,

---

[1] Pages 603, 604. See also *The Magazine of American History*, New York, 1893, vol. xxix. pp. 371–380.

who had befriended him in the Parliament of 1624, had been dead several years; but having an entire confidence in the family he made himself known to Mr. John Ferrar, who received him with all respect, conducted him to a private house at Coppinford, where he slept, went thence to Stamford, and thence to the Scotch army.' Second, that the last time Charles I. came to Titchfield he came to it as a place of refuge in November, 1647. This unfortunate king had been a friend, to a certain extent at least, to our original body politic at a time when our founders needed such a friend; and it may be that during this visit he held these precious volumes in his royal hands. He was beheaded on February 9, 1649, and the fourth Earl of Southampton was " one of the four who were permitted to pay the last solemn duties, in darkness and privacy, to the royal remains." After the restoration, Charles II. invested the earl with the Order of the Garter, and appointed him to be a member of the royal council for foreign plantations. He died May 26, 1667, at Southampton House, near Holborn, London, where the court of the Virginia Corporation had frequently met in former times, and was buried at Titchfield, in Hampshire, where these volumes were preserved.

He left no male heir, Elizabeth Lady Noel, his eldest daughter, inheriting Titchfield. His second daughter, who married secondly the unfortunate

Lord William Russell, is known in history, to which her life contributed a beautiful page, as "the Lady Rachel Russell." Pennant, in his "Account of London," in his description of Southampton House, gives a very touching account of Lady Rachel and Lord William Russell. He says: "The last scene is beyond the power of either pen or pencil. In this house they lived many years. When his lordship passed by it, on the way to execution, he felt a momentary bitterness of death in recollecting the happy moments of the place. He looked towards Southampton House; the tear started into his eye, but he instantly wiped it away." He was executed in 1683, and whether these precious volumes were purchased by Colonel William Byrd the first or second, it pleases me to believe that they were at times held in the hands of that noble martyr to the liberties of his country, before they were brought to Virginia.

Edward Baron Noel, of Titchfield, first Earl of Gainsborough, died in 1689; his son, Wriothesley, the second earl, died in 1690 without male issue, and it may be that the library at Titchfield was not sold until after his death. I do not know when these copies were brought over to Virginia. Mr. Stith, in his preface, says: "As these Records are a very curious and valuable Piece of the Antiquities of our country, I shall give the Reader an Account of them, which I received,

many years ago, in conversation with Col. Byrd
and Sir John Randolph. I had then no Thoughts
of writing the History of Virginia, and therefore
took less Notice than I otherwise should have
done. However, as I am perhaps the only Person now living, anything acquainted with their
History it will not be improper to give it to the
Reader, as I judge it highly worthy of his knowledge." After a description of the two volumes,
which accords with Wodenoth's description of
the Danvers copies, Stith goes on to write: "This
copy was taken by the Order, and for the Use of
the Earl of Southampton, the Company's Treasurer at that time; who, seeing how things were
going with the Company, had their Records thus
carefully copied and compared, and authentically
attested.[1] Whether his Lordship intended to
stand suit with the King for the Rights and privileges of the Company, or whether he did it only
in vindication of his own and the Company's reputation, is uncertain. However, they were carefully preserved in the family; and as the original
Court-Books were taken from the Company by
the King and Privy Council, and never again
restored to them, that I can find, this is perhaps
the only copy now extant. After the death of
that Earl's son, *the Duke* of Southampton (the

---

[1] The Patriots had these records copied and "authentically attested," because they believed that the Court party would corrupt and falsify the history of their past actions.

worthy partner in the Ministry with the Earl of Clarendon, after the Restoration), which happened in the year 1667, the late Col. Byrd's father [that is, Col. William Byrd the first, born 1653, died 1704], being then in England, purchased them of his Executors for sixty guineas."

Mr. Stith, possibly because he had not taken careful notice in the conversation with Colonel Byrd, is certainly at fault in several of the foregoing statements; he does not state exactly when he thought these volumes were purchased, but the inference is that it was soon after the earl's (not duke's) death in 1667; but the Colonel Byrd whom he says was the purchaser was not then fifteen years old. Mr. Jefferson says the purchaser was Colonel William Byrd the second, who was not born until 1674. Stith evidently wrote from memory of a conversation not carefully noted; Jefferson must have known what Stith had published, and, I do not suppose, would have contradicted Mr. Stith without sufficient cause.

Colonel William Byrd the first (1653–1704) came to Virginia about 1673. As his grandfather, Colonel Thomas Stegge or Stagg, had been an active adherent of the Parliament in 1651, and as he was an active adherent of Bacon the rebel in 1676, it may be inferred that he was personally in full sympathy with the view point of these records. But he married Mary, daughter of Colonel Warham Horsmanden, a great-grandson of Catherine (sister of Sir Thomas) Smith; hence they contained many statements which his son, Colonel William Byrd the second (1674–1744), probably resented. As it was certainly the second Colonel Byrd who first communicated these records to Mr. Stith, his conflicting filial interests may have had opposing effects on his mind, which may have been transmitted by him to Stith, and this may account in part for Stith's conflicting opinions between the influence of these records and the influence of the history licensed by the crown.

Some time after 1747, Colonel William Byrd the third (1728–1777) lent these records to Colonel Richard Bland, who had also copies of some of the documents collected by Sir John Randolph and Mr. Richard Hickman, and these books furnished Bland with much of the material on which he based "An Inquiry into the Rights of the British Colonies," published in 1766. Mr. Hugh Blair Grigsby, in his "Virginia Convention of 1776," says: "What John Selden was in the beginning of the troubles in the reign of Charles the First to the House of Commons, was Richard Bland to the House of Burgesses for thirty years during which he was a member. All during that time on all questions touching the rights and privileges of the colony he was the undoubted and truthful oracle." Thomas Jefferson regarded Colonel Bland as "the wisest man south of James River." He was a great-grandson of Richard Bennet and of John Bland senior, members of the Patriot party in our original body politic; a grand-nephew of John Bland junior (who advocated our original charter rights before Charles I., the Commonwealth, and Charles II.), and of Edward Bland, who in 1652 dedicated his "Discovery of New Brittaine" to Sir John Danvers, the regicide, and a cousin to Giles Bland, who was hanged in 1676 for his part taken in Bacon's Rebellion.

Colonel Richard Bland died October 26, 1776, his library was sold in January following and purchased by Thomas Jefferson. Colonel William Byrd the third died January 1, 1777, and his library was sold in April following to Isaac Zane. Mr. Jefferson in a letter to Colonel Hugh P. Taylor, written on October 4, 1823, after stating that the two volumes of Virginia Court Records which had been used by Stith were then in his library at Monticello, added that these volumes had been bought at the sale of the Earl of Southampton's library by "*Doctor* Byrd, of Westover," that is, Colonel William Byrd the second (1674–1744); but he does not give the date of the purchase. Mr. Jefferson then describes the way by which they came into his own possession. "These volumes happened at the time of the sale [January, 1777] to have been borrowed by Colonel Richard Bland, whose library I bought, and with this they were sent to me. I gave notice of it to Mr. Zane [who bought Colonel Byrd's library in April, 1777]; but he never reclaimed them."

These two volumes came to the Library of Congress, where they now (1900) are, from Mr. Jefferson's library, not with the mass of his books in 1815, but after his death, between the years 1826 and 1830. These original copies of the records of the original of the body politic of this nation are the most precious volumes preserved in the Republic.

CHAPTER VIII

UNDER GEORGE III., 1760-1776

AFTER the restoration of the government of England to the crown in 1660, the original charter rights of Virginia were more or less violated or denied by all kings, and, as Thomas Jefferson well says, "especially by George III."

In 1764 the Council and Burgesses of Virginia sent the celebrated petition to George III., memorial to the House of Lords, and remonstrance to the House of Commons. In 1765 the House of Burgesses of Virginia proclaimed the independence of the people of Virginia from taxation by the Parliament of Great Britain. And these acts mark the beginning in the political mother of the colonies of the final contest for the charter rights of the original of the body politic of this nation.

Mr. Jefferson says: "Till the beginning of our Revolutionary disputes we had but one press in Virginia; and that having the whole business of the government, and no competitor for public favor, nothing disagreeable to the governor could find its way into it. We [the Patriot party] procured William Rind to come from Maryland to publish a free paper." The first issue of this paper appeared in May, 1766. The gag was now, at last, being taken off the press in Virginia, and the colony was soon in open "rebellion" against the crown.

Notwithstanding the fact that the crown had been able to suppress or to obscure the real history of our origin as a nation to such an extent that the information of our Revolutionary leaders in Virginia regarding the movement (especially before 1619) was very incomplete, there is ample evidence that they studied carefully the various manuscript copies of the records, and such other documents of the foundation period — charters, ordinances, orders, constitutions, court proceedings, etc. — as their patriotic forefathers had been able to preserve from destruction by the crown officials; and it is certain that they derived inspiration from them in their determination to secure for themselves and for their posterity the charter rights which had been granted in perpetuity to the founders who, at the expense of their own blood and treasure, unassisted by the crown of England, had secured this country for them. Thus the political effect of Stith's history and of these documents reveal the wisdom of the crown of England — from that point of view — in suppressing so earnestly the true history of our political origin, and in keeping for so long the printing press out of Virginia. For this history and these records were certainly instrumental in opening the eyes of our people, and thus clearing the way for our Revolution which secured, finally, the charter rights — the political principles — upon which this nation was founded.

The Virginia courts, which had first managed the business at the capital of the corporation in London, had been suppressed by the crown, and in their room the colony had been under the management of various commissions, committees of the Privy Council, boards of trade, etc.; but the government in the country, as granted to the settlers and citizens of the country, had remained very nearly on the lines instituted therefor in the original "seminary of sedition." When our forefathers began the final struggle for their charter rights, the successors to the old Virginia courts in London were suppressed by them, and in their room "the management of the business" was resumed by another popular court, which the crown probably regarded as another "Seminary for a seditious Parliament," which met on September 5, 1774, at the new capital, Philadelphia, within the ancient bounds of the original corporation. The members of this political body began their work of redress, not by initiating new ideas, but by simply standing upon the monuments which had been erected by their forefathers in the past, and claiming the rights which had descended to them from the founders. Although the Declaration of Independence was attended with a decisive change in the condition of the new states in regard to their external dependence on the crown of Great Britain, their interior organization underwent but little change. New governments were constituted in the several states to take the place of those which had fallen with the colonial régime; but they were formed upon the model of those which previously existed and which had been originated under the authority derived from the charters of 1609, 1612, and 1629, and based on the "English constitution as taken and interpreted, in the most ample and beneficial manner," to the political bodies which founded the colonies.

The patriots of our Revolution did not profess to be planting the seed of our popular course of government. They were protecting the great tree, which had grown from that seed in this country, from the axe of the royal woodmen. Thomas Jefferson in his autobiography, in reference to the debate of June 8–10, 1776, over a declaration of independence, says: " On the other [the Patriot] side, it was urged by J. Adams, Lee, Wythe, and others . . . that the question was not whether by a Declaration of Independence we should make ourselves what we are not, but whether we should declare a fact which already exists :

" That, as to *the people* or *Parliament* of England, *we had always been independent of them*, their restraints on our trade deriving efficacy from our acquiescence [*consent*] only, and not from any rights they possessed of imposing them, and that so far, our connection had been *federal only*, and was now dissolved by the commencement of hostilities."

The following passage, which, for diplomatic reasons, was omitted from our Declaration of Independence, deserves especial notice in considering the source of our political origin. Mr. Jefferson wrote : " We have reminded them [our British brethren] of the circumstances of our emigration and settlement here ; . . . that *these were effected at the expense of our own blood and treasure unassisted by the wealth or the strength of Great Britain ;* that in constituting indeed our several forms of government, we had adopted one common king, thereby laying a foundation for perpetual league and amity with them; but that submission to their Parliament was no part of our Constitution. . . . We might have been a free and a great people together; but a communication of grandeur and of freedom, it seems, is below their dignity. Be it so, since they will have it. The road to happiness and to glory is open to us too. We will tread it apart from them."

Mr. Edward Rider, a member of the Patriot party in the Virginia Corporation, who had settled a plantation in Virginia, was bold enough to tell the Court party in 1623, even after James I. had determined to annul the charters of the Virginia Corporation, that "there was a material difference between the Spanish and English plantations. For the Spanish colonies were founded by the kings of Spain [that is, by the agents, or officials of the kings], out of their own treasury and revenues, and they maintain the garrisons there, together with a large Navy, for their use and defence; whereas the English plantations had been at first settled and since supported at the charge [expense] of private adventurers and planters," — that is, by the original body politic.

The outline which I have given from 1625 to 1776 is sufficient to show that the political principles which inspired Sir Edwin Sandys and the

Patriots of 1608–1609 to determine to obtain the charter rights which would enable them to establish in America a place of refuge for their posterity from "the absolute tyranny then aimed at in Great Britain by the king and Court party," never died out in Virginia. I will add that ancestors of nearly all of her Revolutionary leaders were among the men of genius who petitioned for the charters to the Virginia Corporation of 1609 and 1612, or among the planters who inaugurated the reform movement in America during 1610–1618, or among the members of the First House of Burgesses of 1619, or of the General Assembly which asserted their charter rights before the royal commissioners in 1624; and it is evident that the political purposes which inspired these forefathers continuing as an inheritance to influence their posterity finally sustained Thomas Jefferson and the Patriots of 1775–1776, when they asserted that it was their opposition to the king's direct object to obliterate our charter rights and to establish an absolute tyranny over these states, which caused them to determine to secure, by a complete separation from the crown, the rights formerly granted under the broad seal of England in perpetuity to the original of the body politic of this nation.

In this connection it is very interesting to find among the honorable minority in the House of Lords, who were favorable to American liberty in 1774-75, the dukes of Portland, of Devonshire, and of Northumberland, each of whom descended from Henry Wriothesley, the third Earl of Southampton, and last treasurer of the Virginia Corporation; as is also the fact that the lord mayor, aldermen, and livery of London, whose predecessors had nourished the infant at birth, now delivered in behalf of the sturdy youth an address and remonstrance to the king, marked by such manly freedom as to bring down upon them an indecent royal rebuke for giving encouragement to rebellion.

CHAPTER IX

OF BOUNDARY RIGHTS

IN order to bring out the cause of the historic wrong more clearly, I have given a brief outline of the contest over the popular charter rights. For the same reason I will now call attention in a very brief way to the contest over the vast boundary rights.

The Court party asserted in the controversies of 1623-1624 that in annulling " the company's charters there was no other intention than merely and only the reforming of the company's popular course of government;" but this was not true. James I. not only wished to annul the political rights which he had granted in perpetuity, but under the pretext that the country had been secured under his charter of 1606, and that the enterprise under the popular charters had failed, he was determined to take for the crown the large boundary rights which he had granted in perpetuity to a corporation and body politic, and which had been secured by that body at the expense of their own blood and treasure unassisted by the revenues of the crown.

It was a matter not only of personal pride to James I., but also of great pecuniary as well as political importance to the crown to annul the charters of 1609 and 1612, and to maintain that the colony and the bounds thereof had been established by the company under the royal charter of 1606. James I. died before carrying out the colonial plans which he was formulating. Charles I. finally yielded to the planters many of their original political rights; but " being of the same judgment that his late dear father was " in this matter, he was determined to carry out the purpose of his father against the large boundary rights.

In 1629, under the pretext that the Virginia colony had been secured under the royal charter of 1606, Charles I. granted to Sir Robert Heath and others lands south of the southern boundary of the grant under that charter; and in June, 1632, he granted to Lord Baltimore lands north of the northern boundary of the Virginia grant under that charter. Virginians at once sent remonstrances against the infractions of their boundary rights, continued to protest against the injustice of these grants as well as against all subsequent such like grants, and continued to affirm that the definite bounds were secured under the charter of 1609. And these boundary rights were never yielded by Virginians until the adoption of the Virginia Constitution on July 5, 1776, when Virginia ceded, released, and forever confirmed [not to *the crown* of England, but] to *the people* of Maryland, Pennsylvania, North and South Carolina [her sister colonies, now joined with her in the final contest for charter rights] the territories contained within their charters; but the western and northern extent of Virginia was still " to stand in all other respects as fixed by the Charter of King James I. in 1609, and by the public treaty of peace between the Courts of Britain and France in the year 1763."

It is true that other nations encroached upon this territory, but their title thereto was not acknowledged by our people. Our rights were defended by Washington in the French and Indian war, by Andrew Lewis in Dunmore's war, and by George Rogers Clarke in the Revolution. It is true that by the treaty of 1783 Great Britain only ceded the portion east of the Mississippi, because the rest was claimed by France and Spain; but our people still claimed the original North and South Virginia boundary as "the territory of the United States west of the Mississippi," and they did not rest until they secured it — in good measure. Jefferson paid France the nominal price of about two cents per acre for her claim in 1803; Tyler annexed Texas in 1845; and Scott and Taylor took the balance from Mexico in 1846–1848, — since when it has been under a popular course of government such as the first proprietors wished to have inaugurated therein.

PART IV

An outline of what has been done both towards perpetuating and towards correcting the historic wrong since the loyal political point of view was reversed in 1776.

CHAPTER I

THOMAS JEFFERSON AS A LABORER IN THE FIELD OF ORIGINAL RESEARCH

I HAVE shown in Part I. that James I. resolved to obliterate the popular course of government which the Patriot party was establishing in America; and in Part II. that he was also resolved to suppress the real history of the movement under which this reform government was being instituted in America.

In Part I. and Part III. I have outlined the constant contest — sometimes active, sometimes dormant, but never dead — between the Court and Patriot parties, over these political rights from 1609 to 1776. I believe that the Patriot party — the advocates of a more free government — were always in the majority in Virginia; but the Court party, nearly always, had an absolute control over the evidence, the printing press, and the histories, both in England and Virginia, to such an extent that although the original political rights were absolutely secured to the body politic by the Revolution of 1774–1783, the loyal view-point of our earliest history really reversed, and both cases decided in this country by the proper tribunal, the people; and by the court of last resort, the arbitrament of arms, against the ideas and contentions of the Court party as expressed in their royal edicts, orders, reports, and in the histories licensed by the crown — the historical rights of our founders were not secured. The crown had suppressed the authentic evidences at once so completely, and had continued to exercise such an absolute control over the records and the press in Virginia for so long, that no accounts of our origin were available to the public, which gave a full and fair idea thereof. And thus it came to pass that through the medium of the histories published under the auspices of the crown, which had always been available, we have continued to rob our founders of their historic rights even under the Republic.

I now wish to give an outline of what has been done in the matter of this historic wrong since 1776.

Probably no man deserves more credit for services rendered his country than Thomas Jefferson, and among these services his efforts to collect and preserve our ancient records, and thus to rescue our past history from oblivion, were certainly not the least. William Waller Hening, the editor of "The Statutes at Large . . . of Virginia," was under paramount obligations to him, and in acknowledging these obligations in 1809 he wrote as follows: "It is a melancholy truth that, though we have existed as a nation but little more than 200 years, our public offices are destitute of official documents. It is to the pious care of individuals only that posterity will be indebted for those lasting monuments which perpetuate the oppressions of the kings of England and the patient suffering of the colonists." He continued, to the effect — 'When we review the arbitrary conduct of James I., the equally unjust proceedings of Charles I. and his successors, till resistance became indispensable, we shall cease to wonder that so few evidences of their turpitude have been suffered to remain. What was left undone by the predecessors of George III. was consummated during his reign. All the papers except a few fragments within the reach of his myrmidons were, with more than a savage barbarity of the Goths and Vandals, committed to the flames.' Hening then goes on to say that "Thomas Jefferson has contributed more than any other individual to the preservation of our ancient laws."

As I have frequently said, the especial objects of the crown in the case treated of had been: *First*, to stamp out the political principles which the Virginia Corporation first planted in America. The part taken by Jefferson in righting this wrong is well known. *Second*, to obliterate the true history of the first planting of those principles — of our origin as a nation. The part taken by Jefferson towards righting this wrong may not be so well known, but it was decided. He was as active in securing and preserving evidences in justification of our Revolution as George Chalmers was in collecting and publishing the evidences of the Court party to show that our Revolution was an uncalled-for revolt; and although the crown had been confiscating and destroying the class of evidence which Jefferson wished to find, for one hundred and fifty years, he collected and was able to preserve more of it than any other individual in the Republic.

About the year 1722, Sir John Randolph, a royal official, but a native of Virginia, with the assistance of Mr. Richard Hickman, clerk of the secretary's office, began collecting copies of the important papers from our oldest records then preserved in the colony. "From which evidences," said Stith, "Sir John purposed to write a Preface to our Laws and therein to give an Historical Account of our Constitution and Government; but was prevented from prosecuting it to effect by his many and weighty Publick Employments." Some of the old records preserved by Sir John Randolph were given by his son, the Hon. Peyton Randolph, to Jefferson before the Revolution began. The Hon. Peyton Randolph, the first president of our Congress, died in Philadelphia on October 22, 1775. His library was appraised on January 5, 1776, at £250, and a large portion of it was soon after purchased from his executors by Thomas Jefferson — including about ten manuscript volumes, mostly acts of Assembly, etc., but a good deal else, of an historical character; one book especially, containing evidences of the Virginia Corporation of 1609–1624. All of these books are now preserved in the Library of Congress.

Besides the copies (2 vols.) of the Virginia Court records (1619–1624) used by Stith and already sketched, Jefferson purchased at least *two* other manuscript volumes of the company's records with the Bland library in 1777, — *first*, a large folio volume, lettered " Virginia Company Papers and Records, 1621–1625 " — which Mr. Jefferson has characterized in a note thus: " Letters, Proclamations, Patents, in 1622, 1623; Correspondence, 1625. Transactions in Council and Assembly — their petitions and his Majesty's answer." The writing in this volume, like that in the two volumes of the Virginia Court records, is in the ancient handwriting of the time of James I.[1] *Second.* A smaller volume of copies in the plain handwriting of the 18th century,

[1] There are copies in the plain handwriting of the eighteenth century of these three volumes in the library of " The Virginia Historical Society " at Richmond, Va. They were preserved by John Randolph, of Roanoke, and were probably originally copied by Mr. Hickman for Sir John Randolph.

lettered, " Virginia Papers, 1606 to 1683; " and marked in Mr. Jefferson's handwriting, " never printed."

There is more of the regular record of our original body politic to be found in five of the above mentioned volumes — which were preserved for about fifty years by Mr. Jefferson, before they passed to the Library of Congress, where they now are — than has yet been found in any other repository of evidences.

CHAPTER II

JEFFERSON'S "NOTES ON VIRGINIA"

It is interesting and important to consider the circumstances under which these " Notes " were written. After Jefferson's escape from the troops of Captain McLeod, of Tarleton's command, at Monticello, on June 4, 1781, he went to his seat, " Poplar Forest," in Bedford County, where, riding over his farm, he was thrown from his horse and seriously injured. While thus confined he occupied himself with answering the queries of Mons. De Marbois, which answers were first published in Paris, France, in 1784, under the title, " Notes on the State of Virginia; " and this was the first book bearing on our subject published after the Revolution.

As illustrating the effect of politics even on

our Revolutionary history, it may be noted that Jefferson's political opponents asserted that he was thrown from his horse on Carter's Mountain, Albemarle, in a headlong flight from Tarleton, and not after he had arrived at "Poplar Forest." Jefferson himself refers to these charges in the "Advertisement" to a subsequent edition of the "Notes," wherein he writes: "The subjects are all treated imperfectly; some scarcely touched on. To apologize for this by developing the circumstances of the time and place of their composition, would be to open wounds which have already bled enough." Only yesterday I read in a Virginia paper one of these *ex parte* tales or "campaign lies," which still survives, to the effect that 'Jefferson was thrown from his horse while riding through the blind paths of Carter's Mountain; taken to the house of Mr. Thomas Farrar, on Rockfish River, where he remained two weeks; and was then carried to a cave in the bluff below Scottsville, Albemarle County, Virginia, where he lay concealed for months, being supplied with food by his brother, who lived across James River, at Snowden.' Fortunately for Jefferson's memory, his political opponents did not have an absolute control over the evidences, and there remains ample evidence to refute these stories, even if it is impossible to suppress them.

Although Jefferson, when he wrote these

"Notes" in 1781 and 1782, had secured but little more of the evidence regarding the colonial movement of 1606–1624 than Stith had when writing his history in 1746, he took a more uniformly patriotic view of the event. He did not have enough of the evidences of the Patriots to enable him to restore their obliterated history; but he felt to the full the immortal principles which had inspired them. He had not one of the publications of the managers of the business, and comparatively few of their records, with the exception of those after 1618. In his reply to Query XXIII. he mentions only the four printed histories which I have noticed,—Smith's, Beverley's, Keith's, and Stith's. His " Notes," having been written at " Poplar Forest," in Bedford County, and his library being "at Monticello," in Albemarle, may account for some omissions. In his " Chronological Catalogue of American State Papers," he does not mention all that were known to him; but he mentions enough to show the character of the evidences on which his own opinions had been based. Evidently depending on his memory in reply to Query XIII., he says:[1] James I. executed "*a grant to Sir Thomas Gates and others, bearing date the 9th of March, 1607.*" He evidently had on his mind and really referred to three documents, copies of each of which were then at

[1] Richmond Edition, 1853, p. 119.

Monticello: *First*, "a grant to Sir Thomas Gates and others," of April 10 (o. s.), 1606; *second*, the King's Articles, Instructions and Orders of November 20 (o. s.), 1606; and *third*, the King's Ordinance and Constitution, "bearing date the 9th of March, 1607;" the first being the royal charter of 1606; the second and third contain the original form of government for the colonies designed by James I. Mr. Jefferson then goes on to say: "Of *this grant* [these grants?], however, no particular notice need be taken, as it was [they were?] superseded by letters patent of the same King of May 23 [o. s.], 1609." He then gives an outline of his reading of this first charter to our original body politic, and, after referring to the charter of 1612, says: "In pursuance of the authorities given to the Company by these Charters, and more especially of that part in the Charter of 1609, which authorized them to establish a form of government, they on the 24th of July [August 3d N. s.], 1621, by charter under their common seal," proceeded to establish a liberal form of government which Jefferson outlines.[1] The reference was to the constitution brought by Wyatt to Virginia, in October, 1621; but as stated in the land grant from Sir Francis Wyatt to Thomas Hothersall, dated February 5, 1622 (N. s.), once recorded in the

[1] Richmond Edition, 1853, p. 120.

Virginia Land Office Records, Book No. 1, page 1 (now torn out), our government was established on "The Great Charter of Laws and Orders," issued by the Virginia Quarter Court under authority derived from the charters of 1609 and 1612, bearing date at London, November 28 (N. S.), 1618, and instituted in Virginia under Sir George Yeardley, in 1619.

Under the impression, it seems, that the Virginia Corporation and body politic was an ordinary company he gives his idea of the dissolution of "the company," as follows:[1] "The king and the company quarrelled, and by a mixture of law and force the latter were ousted of all their rights, without retribution, after having expended £100,000 [say $2,500,000 present value] in establishing the colony, without the smallest aid from the government. King James suspended their powers by proclamation of July 15 [o. s.], 1624, and Charles I. took the government into his own hands. Both sides had their partisans in the colony; but, in truth, the people of the colony in general thought themselves little concerned in the dispute. There being three parties interested in these several charters, what passed between the first and second it was thought could not affect the third. If the king seized on the powers of the company, they only passed into other hands, without increase or diminution, while

[1] Richmond edition, 1853, p. 121.

the rights of the people remained as they were. But they did not remain so long. The northern parts of their country were granted away to the Lords Baltimore and Fairfax," etc. Jefferson evidently knew of the contests of the people over land rights, but did not know of their earlier contests for their political rights. As I have said, Jefferson did not have enough of the evidence of the Patriots to enable him to restore their obliterated history, and the idea conveyed by him of " the dissolution " is not accurate. We are now more familiar with the " quarrel," or contest, between the crown and the Virginia Corporation. We know that the people in the colony were vitally concerned in the dispute, and without doubt would have felt it more deeply if James I. had lived longer. " The three parties," to whom Jefferson alludes, were the king (the crown), the adventurers in England (whom he regarded as the company), and the planters in Virginia ; but the last two really composed one body politic (the people), who had secured the country at their own expense, and of these two the planters were more directly concerned in the political rights than the adventurers. They well knew the value of those rights, and continued to contend for, and to petition for, them from 1624 to 1776, when they determined to secure them, and did so.

Mr. Jefferson's imperfect treatment of some

phases of this movement was owing to the circumstances of the place and time of the composition of these "Notes," as well as to the lack of authentic evidences; but taking all things into consideration his ideas regarding the case of our founders were remarkably correct.

CHAPTER III

AN OUTLINE OF WHAT WAS DONE UNDER THE REPUBLIC FROM 1784 TO 1861 TOWARDS PERPETUATING THE HISTORIC WRONG COMMITTED BY JAMES I. AND THE COURT PARTY IN 1624; AND WHAT WAS DONE TOWARDS CORRECTING THAT WRONG

As nearly all of the numerous books, in the premises, published from 1784 to 1861, were based on the crown evidences, it will not be possible to give here more than the merest outline of what has been done since 1784 toward perpetuating the ideas of our origin as a nation which were disseminated under the auspices of the crown. Portions of the works of Captain John Smith, the historian licensed by the crown, were made still more available by reprints issued in the Republic as early as 1819, and repeatedly thereafter in 1833, 1837, 1838, 1845, etc. Over a dozen laudatory biographies of this historian, and histories "too numerous to mention," have been published in this country since the Revolution, all based largely on his books, and of course all of these — reprints, biographies, and histories — have aided in perpetuating the purpose of James I. and the Court party to obliterate the real history of the original of the body politic of this nation. It is not my purpose to review these books; they must be judged by their fruit.

The first book published in England under the crown,[1] written even partially from the political view point of the Patriot party, was Peckard's "Life of Nicholas Ferrar," printed in 1790, after the colonies had secured their charter rights. It was based on the memoirs, already mentioned, written by John Ferrar about 1655, providentially preserved, and handed down in manuscript from father to son. The old deputy gave them to his son John in 1657, who left them to his son Edward, who gave them to his son Edward, who died in 1769, after having given them to his son-in-law, the Rev. Peter Peckard, who finally published them.

In 1823 "The New Life of Virginia," which was first published in 1612, was republished by the Massachusetts Historical Society, being, I believe, the first reprint in the Republic of one of the original publications of the managers of the business. In June, 1839, "The Southern Liter-

[1] Wodenoth's book was published under the Commonwealth in 1651.

ary Messenger," Richmond, Va., published John Rolfe's " Relation to James I. of the State of Virginia in 1607-1616," from the copy, preserved in the Royall MSS., which had passed into the British Museum, being, I believe, the first one of the original manuscript accounts by a contemporary manager of the business in the colony printed in Virginia.

" Nova Britannia," first published in 1609, was first reprinted in this country by Peter Force in 1836. " A True Declaration," of 1610, and " A Declaration," of 1620, were first reprinted by Peter Force in 1844. Thus, after the ideas of the Court party had been impressed on the minds of our people for over two hundred years, a few of the publications of the managers became available to the public in the United States.

Anderson's " History of the Colonial Church," published in England in 1845, gave some extracts from Wingfield's " Discourse of Virginia; " the whole was first printed in this country by Mr. Charles Deane, of Cambridge, Massachusetts, in 1859. A portion of Strachey's manuscript, " Historie of Travaile into Virginia Britannia," and a letter from the Lord De la Warr, governor of Virginia, written at Jamestown, July 17, 1610, were printed for the Hakluyt Society, London, 1849. Birch's "Court and Times of James the First," published in London in 1849, contains many contemporary letters referring to this movement, which had not been available to the public before. An account of the first General Assembly (August 9-14, 1619) ever convened in America was published for the first time in 1857 in the "Collections" of the New York Historical Society. The official reports of this most important Assembly were probably destroyed (they have not been found) both in England and in Virginia; but under Providence Mr. John Pory sent an account of the proceedings by Marmaduke Rayner, the pilot of a Dutch man-of-war (a ship under commission from the Prince of Orange), which left Virginia in the autumn of 1619, to Sir Dudley Carleton, then in Holland. Carleton — he was created Viscount Dorchester in 1628 — died in 1632, and his papers finally passed in the 18th century into the Public Record Office in London, where this document is now preserved.

Documents discovered (and published, and discovered, and not yet published) since 1850 are too numerous to mention particularly. The examples given are sufficient to illustrate the various ways by which evidences have been providentially preserved.

In 1856 the State of New York published in the first volume of documents relating to the colonial history of that colony several papers which gave to the public the first idea of the real interest taken in the first English colony by the United States of the Netherlands. In 1858 Lord De la Warr's "Relation," of 1611, was privately reprinted in London.

In 1857–1859 the British government published the "Calendar of the State Papers, Domestic Series," of the reign of James I. (1603–1625) in four volumes; and in 1862, the "Calendar of State Papers, Colonial Series, East Indies," etc. (1513–1616). Each of these five volumes locate papers having reference to the English colonies in America.

In 1860, the "Calendar of State Papers, Colonial Series" (1574–1660), which relate entirely to the American colonies, was published. This is a very important volume. Many of these papers had come to the state paper department of the Public Record Office of Great Britain from various repositories of crown officials or offices, and therefore had been preserved under the auspices of the crown from the first; but many others have come into the Record Office or the British Museum since 1625 from repositories of a private character. The documents listed in these calendars and in the various catalogues of the British Museum relative to our subject, have to be analyzed with great care. Many of them were issued directly from the crown — Privy Council, royal courts, commissions, etc. Many of a political character were written by or to the king, the members of his Privy Council, or other royal officials, and thus many are as partisan in character and unjust to the *vis vitæ* of our foundation and to the intentions of our founders as is the history licensed by the crown. But some of the evidences — and especially among those which have come in since 1625 from other sources than the crown repositories — are nonpartisan, valuable, and reliable evidences.

In 1860 there was printed for the Camden Society in England the "Letters from George Lord Carew to Sir Thomas Roe," 1615–1617, which conveyed to this English ambassador at the court of the Great Mogul some of the latest Virginia news. In the same year there was published at Albany, New York, a reprint of Hamor's "A True Discourse," etc. (1615); and in the "Transactions and Collections of the American Antiquarian Society," vol. iv., "Newport's Discoveries in Virginia" (1607), three papers, edited by E. E. Hale, A. M., and Wingfield's "A Discourse of Virginia," edited by Charles Deane, A. M.

A decided interest was developing in our earliest history, which might have brought forth good fruit long ago, save for the obstructions incidental to the civil war and to the political influences resulting therefrom.

CHAPTER IV

AN OUTLINE OF THE ORIGIN OF THE SO-CALLED "JOHN SMITH CONTROVERSY" FROM 1860 TO 1885

IN my effort to correct the historic wrong committed under James I., I have given a particular account of, or reprints of, many of the prints and manuscripts written during 1606–1616, and found since 1865, in "The Genesis of the United States" and "The First Republic in America," and in the latter book I have referred to many written after 1616 which have been found both before and since 1865. Therefore it is not necessary to continue the outline of what has been done towards perpetuating or correcting the historic wrong of 1624 since our civil war (1865). But it is necessary to give an outline of the beginning of the so-called "John Smith controversy."

Wingfield's "A Discourse of Virginia" (1608), edited by Mr. Charles Deane, of Cambridge, Massachusetts, was first printed in Boston in 1859, and afterwards included in the collections of the American Antiquarian Society printed in 1860. In his notes, Mr. Deane questioned Smith's veracity as to "the Pocahontas incident." He was soon replied to by Ex-Governor Wyndham Robertson, of Virginia (a descendant from Pocahontas), in a paper on "The Marriage of Pocahontas," read before "The Virginia Historical Society," and afterwards published in "The Virginia Historical Reporter," vol. ii. part i. pp. 67-87 (Richmond, 1860), and in "The Historical Magazine" (New York), for October, 1860. And the controversy thus begun has been going on ever since.

Of course little was done in the matter of past history during the civil war (1861-1865). In 1866 Mr. Charles Deane had Smith's "A True Relation of Virginia" (1608) reprinted, and in his notes thereon he again questioned the accuracy of Smith's account of his life having been saved by Pocahontas. Mr. Deane's so-called "attack on Captain John Smith" is almost confined to this incident. In most other things he was disposed to accept Smith's estimate of himself and of others; he regarded Smith as "the master spirit of the colony of Virginia," and, giving no consideration to the political conditions obtaining in 1624, was disposed to accept Smith's account of the Virginia movement from 1606 to 1624.

Mr. Henry Adams continued the controversy in the "North American Review" for January, 1867, sustaining Mr. Deane.

Since Stith published his history in 1747 nearly all historians of Virginia during the period —

1606–1624 — have rejected some of the more important ideas conveyed by Smith's history. While accepting Smith's account implicitly for the period prior to 1618, they rejected much of it after that date. While accepting his praise of himself at all times, they generally rejected or smoothed over his harsh criticism of others. In 1869 the Rev. Edward D. Neill published his "Virginia Company of London," in which he reversed the old treatment of the case by rejecting Smith's praise of himself, and accepting much of his harsh criticism of others. Smith's veracity can be tested as well by his account of events after 1618 as before; as well by his references to others as by his references to himself. Both the old treatment of the case and Mr. Neill's are self-contradictory. Neither side had given due consideration to the political conditions then obtaining, and consequently the reform movement and its managers had suffered accordingly on both sides. It was now evident that there was something radically wrong somewhere with our earliest history. The controversy was no longer confined to the Pocahontas incident; it became broader and broader as the inquiry progressed.

Hon. W. W. Henry, of Virginia, took up the discussion in an article in defense of Smith, published in "Potter's American Monthly" in 1875. The controversy was continued in "A History of American Literature" (1607–1676), in 1878, by Professor Moses Coit Tyler, who rejects Smith's account of being saved by Pocahontas, but defends him in many other respects. Edward Eggleston and Lillie Eggleston Seelye entered the controversy in 1879, in an extended account of Smith, published under the title of "Pocahontas," in which "the incident" is accepted, as it were, with a proviso. In the same year Mr. John Fiske came to the defense of Smith in a lecture at University College, London, England. The matter was also considered, *pro* and *con*, about this time, by Hon. George Bancroft, Bryant and Gay, Hon. Henry Cabot Lodge, Henry Stevens, General Sir J. Henry Lefroy, and others.

In 1881 Mr. Charles Dudley Warner published 'A Study of Smith's Life and Writings,' in which he did not accept Smith at his own estimate of himself. Considering the facts that Mr. Warner did not have all the evidences in the case before him, and that he did not take into consideration the effect of politics on the case, his estimate of Smith and of his writings was probably as near correct as could be expected. But though he did not accept Smith at his own estimate, he was too much disposed to accept others at Smith's estimate of them.

On February 24, 1882, Hon. W. W. Henry delivered an address before the Virginia Historical Society on "The Settlement at Jamestown, with particular reference to the late attacks upon

Captain John Smith, Pocahontas, and John Rolfe."
Mr. Henry's address was largely based on mistaken ideas derived from crown evidences. He thought that Smith's history had been written at the instance of the Virginia Company of London; that it was accepted as the standard history of the colony from its first appearance; that for more than two hundred and fifty years, "if we except Thomas Fuller," no one had discredited Smith until the year 1860, when Mr. Charles Deane, of Massachusetts, did so. As a matter of fact, the history was not written at the instance of the company, and it is manifest that the Patriot party could never have accepted this "history," licensed by the crown in 1624, as a real history of their enterprise. "*Nequid non veri audeat, nequid veri non audeat.* The great task for an historian is the ascertainment of truth, which when once found he dare not conceal and be true to his calling;" and it has always been incumbent on historians to be certain that the history which the Court party licensed was not impeached by the records which the Court party suppressed, before they regarded the censored story as reliable authority, or considered it as a real history.

Although Mr. Deane was, I believe, the first modern historian to question Smith's veracity as to the Pocahontas incident, Smith's history had really been impeached, and the author's veracity questioned, more or less, by every record of the

Virginia Company which had been found, and by every historian of Virginia since Stith.

Mr. Henry gave no consideration to the past politics, which really controlled the history as well as most of the evidence which he was relying upon; yet he showed that he knew the power of such influence by appealing to sectional politics and setting in motion that prejudice in support of his argument. An appeal to present prejudices in a question of over two hundred and fifty years ago is really a confession of judgment, and it is more apt to be made for the purpose of concealing than for revealing historic facts; but many people are more apt to be influenced by prejudices than by facts, and therefore these prejudices have been appealed to by some of the advocates of the licensed historian in this controversy ever since. I had been making a study of the case of our founders for some time, when Mr. Henry's address appeared. I was not prepared to enter the discussion, but I did not wish to see a sectional matter made of this important historical question, and I protested against that mode of treating the case in "The Richmond Dispatch" of March 9, 1882.

Mr. J. A. Doyle, in his "English Colonies in America," published in 1882, treated the question very much as Deane, Palfrey, Tyler, and some others had done. He rejected the Pocahontas incident, regarded other portions of

Smith's story as untrue or extravagant, and yet took a favorable view of Smith's character.

In 1883 "The adventures and discourses of Captain John Smith . . . newly ordered by John Ashton," appeared, in which Smith's whole story is accepted as true and fustianized upon by Ashton. John Esten Cooke's "Virginia," was also published this year. Mr. Cooke devotes about 145 pages to the plantation of Virginia during 1606–1624; giving about 27 pages per annum to the period of the king's government, 1607–1609, and about 4 pages per annum to the period of the corporation and body politic, 1610–1624. He defended Smith very warmly, but his account is largely based on evidences licensed by the crown, and he gave no consideration to the effect of politics on these evidences. He regarded James I. as a narrow minded, obstinate man, of little ability; yet he wrote the earlier portion of his history almost entirely on the evidences of the licensed historians of James I.

In 1884 Mr. Edward Arber, in his "English Scholar's Library," published a complete edition of Captain John Smith's works. Mr. Arber gives some other evidences, and mentions many more; but evidently based his opinions almost entirely on the "Works" which he was editing; had a very strong reliance on their historic value, and a great admiration for the author. Consequently he had no idea of the special importance of the movement his author pretended to be describing.

Mr. Arber gave no consideration to the political conditions which controlled the publications he was reprinting; but if he had done so, as a loyal subject of the crown of Great Britain, he would naturally have been more apt to take the view of the history licensed by the crown, than would a loyal advocate of the popular course of government, the history of the institution of which in this country the crown wished to obliterate. He seems to have been under the impression that the question as to the veracity of Smith's history depended solely on the accuracy of the Pocahontas incident, and that too much had been made of that Pocahontas matter.

It is not in the scope of this book to continue the outline of "the John Smith controversy" — or rather, the controversy over the treatment of our foundation and founders under the auspices of James I. and the Court party — down to the present time; but in the interest of the task which I have undertaken it was necessary to call attention to the important fact that since the civil war, in order to support the history licensed by the crown, and thus perpetuate the original historic wrong, an appeal has been made to the influence of sectional politics (which has absolutely no bearing on the veracity of Smith's history), and that through this influence the advocates of the history licensed by the crown have exercised almost as absolute a control over our earliest history in Virginia under the Republic as the Court party, through the influence of past politics, formerly exercised under the crown.

CHAPTER V

A PERSONAL EXPLANATION REGARDING MY OWN WORK IN THE FIELD OF OUR EARLIEST HISTORY, DURING 1876-1900

My own work in the field of our earliest history has been so frequently misunderstood and misrepresented that it is necessary for me to explain it more fully than I have yet done.

I have always taken an interest in our history, and I read carefully the various articles and books in the so-called "John Smith controversy," as they came to my hands; but I was not fully satisfied with any of them. Goethe says that "In the works of man, as in those of nature, it is the intention which is chiefly worth studying." I determined to look into the matter for my own information, and in 1876-1877 I made an independent study of the case of our founders, as I found it in books. This study convinced me that there was something radically wrong somewhere with our earliest history as it had been published. In the course of my study the partisan character of the "history" became evident to me; my faith in the honorable "intention" of the work of our founders, at first weak, had grown stronger and stronger, while my former belief in the personal disinterestedness and purity of the "intention" of Captain John Smith's published works grew less and less until it vanished, and it became evident to me that the contemporary histories gave a false idea of the founding and of the founders of my country.

In the books which I had been studying, the purpose of the crown to obliterate the facts had been so completely carried out that I could not say what the true history was; but I was convinced that Smith did not give the true history. I did not know what had caused Smith's history to be accepted in the first instance, or for so long after, as history; but I was convinced that a great historic wrong had been done the real founders of our country by those who wrote it and published it as history, and by those who had continued to accept it as such. The task seemed to me to be a very important one, and a very proper one for a Virginian to undertake; therefore I determined to undertake it — to go regularly to work and try to find out exactly in what the historic wrong consisted, and the causes of it; to correct the wrong and to remove the causes of it, if I could.[1]

[1] See Preface to *The First Republic in America*, p. iv.

I began to labor in the field of original research in 1878; I retired from active business on account of deafness in 1880, and then undertook my task in earnest. Since 1882 I have written from time to time sundry articles for sundry magazines and newspapers, which reveal my views on the questions as those views developed.

In 1890 I published in "The Genesis of the United States" the first fruits of my long research. The chief value of this work lies in the fact that it is especially devoted to giving copies of, or references to, the original evidences written during 1606–1616, and information relative to the members of the body politic of that period, and in the fact that it is the first book published under the Republic with the intention of restoring to that body the honors which they had always been deprived of in our histories. In continuing my research and study, after 1890, I saw that the movement was a political one, and that I was mistaken in some of the opinions which I had given expression to in the book — especially in the biographies. This caused me to reconsider the case, and thus finally to locate correctly the causes of my errors. And it is now important for me, in the interest of my task, to give an explanation of these errors of opinion.

So much concealment of facts and dissemination of false ideas, by those controlling the evidences, had obtained for so long, and naturally so much confusion had followed, that although I knew an historic wrong had been committed, although I had made a careful study of the case, had located some of the errors of omission and of commission, and some of the sources of the wrong, I had not located all of them; consequently I did not fully understand the case myself. I had failed (as every one else had previously done) to give due consideration to the influence of imperial politics on the history of this popular movement. I had also failed to consider properly the absolute control over the evidences, in print and in manuscript, possessed by the crown. And the importance of giving due consideration to these things in these premises cannot be overestimated.

It is true that I protested against Smith's history; but I did so because I knew that a criticism of his peers and a eulogy of a man compiled by himself, or his friends, was not really history. I had given no consideration to the important political facts that the book had been licensed under the crown; had conformed with the political purposes of the Court party, and was not only not history, but was *ex parte* evidence of a very objectionable kind. I had held Smith and his friends solely and personally responsible for the wrong done by his history.

So far from having implicated James I. and the Court party in any way in the matter, I had looked upon them as the great friends of the whole movement, and had regarded the royal manuscript evidences — written by the king, by his Privy Councillors and other royal officials, and by others to the king and to the royal officials — as being official and entirely reliable evidences, when as a matter of fact these evidences are *ex parte*, and almost entirely in accord with the political purposes of the Court party to conceal or obscure — rather than to give — any facts favorable to the political purposes of the opponent Patriot party.

I was also mistaken in thinking that religious influence (in the contest then going on between the Church of England and the Church of Rome) was the chief original cause of the historic wrong. I did not overestimate this influence in the premises, but unfortunately I did not consider the most important influence at all. The paramount, original, and sustaining cause of the wrong was without doubt imperial politics; but church and state were then so close as to be almost inseparable. The officials of both church and state were active in confiscating the evidences of the Virginia body politic after that body had been condemned by the crown, and in disseminating the histories of the acts of that body which had been licensed by the crown.

And the cause of this *ex parte* work on the part of the officials — both of church and of state — was the determination of James I. for political purposes to obliterate the facts regarding the movement. Of the two chief influences inspiring American colonization, the religious may have predominated in New England; but politics was the mother's milk of Virginia. My failure to take into consideration the political conditions then obtaining caused me to misunderstand the true character of the company conducting the movement, and of some of the most important political features of the movement.

As the book related to events prior to 1617, and as I wished to defend our founders of that period from the unjust charges of the contemporary historian, I naturally wrote from the view point of the Sir Thomas Smith party in the corporation; but as I had failed to give proper consideration to the national political conditions then obtaining in England, and to the fact that this party finally affiliated with the national Court party, I was mistaken in some of the opinions expressed of James I., of several members of the Court party, of Sir Edwin Sandys, and of several members of his party.

No party in our country has now an absolute control over evidence such as the Court party had while our country was under the crown;

but even under a free government, with a free press, the influence of party politics on history as published is very great. Under the royal government the influence of imperial politics was paramount. I knew these political facts when compiling "The First Republic in America," in 1897, and therefore, instead of writing that book from the point of view from which I wrote "The Genesis of the United States," or from the view point of the Court party, as had been the custom of historians generally (in whole or in part) from the first, I wrote from the point of view of the Patriot party. This had really always been the correct political view point for the history of this movement, and it had been the loyal view for our historians to take for over one hundred and twenty years; yet "The First Republic in America" has the honor of being the first book so written to be published in the Republic. It was the first effort to restore to our foundation as a nation the inspiring political features of which it was robbed by those who controlled the evidences and the histories under the crown. And there could be no clearer illustration of the very effectual manner in which the purpose of the Court party had been carried out than the fact that this book was condemned in several of our leading historical magazines and reviews, especially because it presented the case of our founders from this loyal, patriotic, and correct point of view rather than from the view of the crown evidences.

So far as I know I was the first person under the Republic to undertake seriously the task of correcting this historic wrong. I had to find my way to the true history, as it were, through a fenny field, filled with pitfalls and other obstacles, without guides, and at the constant risk of being led astray by the unreal light produced by Jack-with-a-lantern. As I had been studying the case for some time before I undertook my task, I knew some of the difficulties; but I had no conception of the magnitude of the opposition with which I should have to contend, nor of the obstacles which I should have to overcome. When I became aware of these things, I saw that my means were too limited for me to have undertaken the task single-handed, but my heart was then in the work, and I could not give it up. Therefore, I determined to make every sacrifice in order to carry out my object, and I have done so.

I have had to contend with the almost insurmountable obstacles placed in the way of finding the facts by James I., his commissioned officials, and licensed historians. I have not only had the disappointments and expenses always incidental to searching for — finding or not finding — evidences; but when found it has frequently been very difficult to obtain complete copies of the manuscripts, and when obtained it has sometimes been very difficult to make a correct analysis of the contents of the documents. If we note the fact that it is not possible to write any book so as to prevent those from finding fault with it who wish to do so, we will see the great difficulty of compiling a book in the best form for correcting the wrong impressions which have resulted from an almost absolute control over the history and all evidences for nearly one hundred and fifty years by the crown officials. After an article or book was written I have had the difficulty of finding a publisher liberal enough and patriotic enough to undertake the publication of an article or a book opposing opinions which have grown gray with age and become popular. Then I have had the difficulty of securing a sufficient number of advance orders to justify the printing of such a book. After publication I have had to confront the opposition arising from the fact that as the crown had suppressed the case so effectually for so long, the history written in opposition to the founding and to the founders of the popular course of government in this country had become the popular history of our national origin. And the case of the crown against our patriotic founders was not only supported by the veneration which age confers, but the advocates of the crown evidences actually brought present sectional politics into play in order to aid them in perpetuating the historic wrong. The true history of our political foundation had been placed under the ban by the officials under the crown; and my effort in behalf of the true history was at once placed under the ban, so far as they could do so, by the advocates of the historians licensed under the crown. The court which licensed the publication of Smith's history would have burnt my books and imprisoned me; but thanks to the immortal principles which inspired our founders, the advocates of John Smith could only "roast" my books and abuse me. Thus it will have been seen that the difficulty has not only been to overcome the obstacles placed in the way by James I. and his successors under the crown, but also those which have grown up in the way, so to speak, under the Republic.

In the interest of the task that I had undertaken, and to offset as far as possible these misrepresentations of my work, I published (and circulated at my own expense) in the fall of 1898 a pamphlet called "The History of our Earliest History; an appeal for the truth of history in vindication of our legitimate origin as a nation, as an act of justice to our founders, and as an incentive to patriotism." For the same purpose I published in "The Virginia Magazine of History and Biography," for January, 1899, 'A note on Mr. W. W. Henry's views of "The First Republic in America."'

When I undertook my task I not only had no idea of the magnitude of the difficulties before me, but I did not have an adequate idea of the magnitude of the historic wrong which had been committed. The importance of my task is now fully realized by those who look at the real controversy from the patriotic point of view. The difficulties remaining in the way of correcting the wrong are not so much with the obstacles which were placed in the way under James I. as with the obstacles resulting therefrom — present obstacles. Every school in which the earliest history of Virginia has been taught has used histories presenting the case largely from the view point, and on the evidences of the Court party; every public, and nearly every private, library in the United States has contained such histories; the ideas of our national foundation and of our political founders have been based on the evidences of the Court party against our patriotic founders for so long that the complete correction of the original historic wrong in every detail, or in the mind of every person, is not now possible; and I have never hoped to accomplish the impossible. We have had no history which presented the case from the view point and on the evidences of the Patriot party; we have not been taught, and our libraries have not contained, such histories; hence very many of our people, who wish to understand the case fully and fairly, have

AN EXPLANATION

not had an opportunity to read the evidences of the Patriot party against the acts of the Court party. I wish to show to these people that an historic wrong was committed by James I., his commissioned officials, and licensed historians; I wish to give to those who want to honor the founders of the popular course of government in our country a true and patriotic history of this movement so far as is now possible; and although I have not always taken the correct political point of view, this has been the "intention" of my work from the first.

The object of this book is to show more clearly than I have yet done the correct political and historical point of view; the real importance of the movement; the political character of the historic wrong done those who, under the charters of 1609 and 1612, inaugurated a popular course of government in this country; the political influences which swayed opinions, evidences, and histories under James I., and the political influences which have been instrumental in upholding the evidences and purposes of the crown ever since. I have tried to make these things clear in Parts I., II., III., and IV.; but a proper understanding of the politics of the movement is essential to a correct understanding of its history. Therefore I will try to give as complete an idea as I can briefly do of its leading political features in the following Part V.

We give thanks to the little acorn for the great oak, and those who planted the seed of our popular course of government in our country must not be forgotten.

PART V

A REVIEW of some of the leading political features in the case between the Patriot party, which managed the business and laid the foundation upon which this great nation has been erected, and the Court party, which controlled the evidences and laid the foundation upon which the history of this great movement has been written.

CHAPTER I

THE IMPORTANCE OF THE MOVEMENT AS REPRESENTED IN THE CROWN EVIDENCES AND AS IT WAS IN FACT

THE first English colony in the present United States — the political mother of the colonies — was not founded by a king; nor by an agent of a king; nor under a form of government designed by a king; nor on the principles advocated by a king and Court party.

James I. did not even risk his royal revenues in founding colonies in Virginia. The efforts to establish colonies by companies and councils under royal government resulted in failure. For the sake of the liberal political charter rights of self-government, etc., granted in perpetuity, a "corporation and body politic" undertook the task at their own expense.

Almost as soon as the body politic had secured a hold on the country, had begun to establish their popular idea of government in the colony, and to settle landed estates in their domain, James I. determined to rob that body of the popular political rights which he had granted in perpetuity under the broad seal of England, and of the property rights which they had secured at the expense of their own blood and treasure, unassisted by the revenues of the crown. In order to justify himself before his people and posterity for doing these dishonorable things, he attempted to prove by sundry "swift witnesses" for the crown — in manuscript and in print — that Virginia had really been founded under "his Majesties first grant of April, 1606, and his Majesty's most prudent and princely instructions,"[1] and that all had gone to ruin under "the popular course of government" instituted by the Patriot party, which the Court party called "misgovernment." In order to justify and to conceal the wrong of this his proceeding, he confiscated the evidences of the corporation and licensed false "histories" of the whole transaction.

John Ferrar correctly said,[2] that "The king was at the bottom of the whole proceeding, which from beginning to end was a despotic violation of honour, and of justice; which proved him to be a man void of every laudable principle of action; a man who in all his exertions made himself the scorn of those who were not in his power, and the detestation of those who were; a man whose head was indeed encircled with the

---

[1] See *The First Republic in America*, pp. 540–542, etc.
[2] See *Memoirs of the Life of Mr. Nicholas Ferrar*, by P. Peckard, D. D., Cambridge (England), 1790, p. 147.

Royal Diadem, but never surely was head more unworthy or unfit to wear it." From the view point of the Patriot party, it was indeed as dishonorable a piece of work as any king was ever guilty of.

The chief agents of James I. in depriving the political body of the charter rights under which the first colony had been founded were his Privy Council; the royal commission of 1623, with Sir William Jones (who had served the king in Ireland) presiding; and the Court of King's Bench, Chief Justice Sir James Ley (who had served the king in Ireland) presiding. The Patriots, however, "laid the great load on" Lionell Cranfield Earl of Middlesex and Lord High Treasurer of England, as being the king's chief instrument in this matter.

The king's chief agents in confiscating the evidences of the corporation and disseminating the manuscript evidences (reports, orders, letters, discourses, documents, etc.) favorable to the purposes of the crown, were his Privy Councilors and royal commissioners of 1623 and 1624. The large commission of July 25, 1624, was especially instrumental in confiscating the evidences, records, etc., of the Virginia Corporation and body politic, being required by the crown to take and to keep all the evidences of all sorts in any ways concerning the colony of Virginia. It was composed of : —

Members of the Privy Council and officials of the crown: Henry Montagu Viscount Mandeville, Lord President of the Council; William Lord Pagett, Arthur Lord Chichester, Sir Thomas Edmonds, Sir John Suckling, Sir George Calvert, Sir Edward Conway, Sir Richard Weston, and Sir Julius Cæsar.

Officials of the Crown: Sir Humfry May, Sir Baptist Hickes, Sir Thomas Smith, Sir Henry Mildmay, Sir Thomas Coventry, and Sir Robert Heath.

Knights: Ferdinando Gorges, Robert Killigrew, Charles Montagu, Philip Carie, Francis Gofton, Thomas Wroth, John Wolstenholme, Nathaniel Rich, Samuel Argall, and Humfry Handford.

Ministers, etc.: Matthew Sutcliff, Dean of Exeter, and Francis White, Dean of Carlisle; Thomas Fanshaw, Esquire, Clerke of the Crown.

Aldermen of London: Robert Johnson, James Cambell, and Raphe Freeman.

Esquires: Morice Abbot, Nathaniel Butler, George Wilmore, William Hackwell, John Mildmay, Philip Jermayne, Edward Johnson, Thomas Gibbes, Samuel Wrote, John Porey, Michaell Hawes, and Edward Pallavacine.

Merchants: Robert Bateman, Martyn Bonde, Thomas Stiles, Nicholas Leate, Robert Bell, Abraham Cartwright, Richard Edwards, John Dyke, Anthony Abdy, William Palmer, Edward

Dichfield, George Mole, and Richard Morer, — fifty-six in all; and quite certainly less than a dozen were then in sympathy with the Patriots. And that they did their work effectually is evident, for not a scrap of the original records of the corporation has been found in England.

His chief agent in disseminating and perpetuating a false idea of the movement was the printing press under the control of the Court of Star Chamber, and of the High Commission, with George Abbot (who had won the confidence of James I. in 1608, by publicly supporting him in the controversy over the Gowrie Plot of 1600), Archbishop of Canterbury, presiding. The chief active agents in these premises were the historians licensed by the crown, Rev. Samuel Purchas and Captain John Smith. The history of the popular reform movement was "corrupted and falsified" by them, and we are still enjoying (?) the fruit of their labors in the Republic founded on the principles which they opposed.

It was probably Purchas rather than Smith whom James I. regarded as the historian of the colonial movements.[1] His summary, an outline of the ideas of the Court party, gives the chief honors to James I., whom he regarded as "beyond comparison compared with others, a meere transcendent; beyond all his Predecessors, Princes of this Realme; beyond the neighbour-

[1] See *The First Republic in America*, p. 636.

ing Princes of his own times, beyond the conceits of subjects dazled with such brightnes: Beyond our victorious Debora not in sex alone, but as Peace is more excellent then War, and Salomon then David. . . . Thus at home doth Great Britain enjoy this Gem of Goodnes, the best part of the Ring of the worlds Greatnes; And abroad, we see that as Gods Steward to others also, His Majestie hath ballanced the neerer World by his prudence, by justice of commerce visited the remoter, by truest fortitude without wrong to any man conquered the furthest North, and by justest temperance disposed the overflowing numbers of his Subjects, not in Intrusions and Invasions of weaker Neighbours, but in the spacious American Regions to breed New Britaines in another World." These things were not done by James I. in person, nor at his expense; but Purchas considered that they were done by his agents or representatives and gave the honors to James I.

It is now certain that James I. was determined to commit a great wrong when he attempted to annul the popular charters conveying the right of self-government and other liberal privileges to the citizens of Virginia. He did not live long enough to actually deprive them of their original political charter rights, yet our forefathers were not able to fully secure those rights from the crown for one hundred and fifty years, and then only by force and arms. And thus this premeditated wrong of James I. was corrected one hundred and twenty years ago.

It is now certain that James I. was determined to commit a great wrong when he attempted to obliterate the true idea and to disseminate a false idea of the origin of this nation. And unfortunately he did live long enough to confiscate the evidences of the political body, to see false "histories" published, and thus to put into effect his plans for obliterating the true history of the whole movement. As a result of this determination of an absolute power, carried out by royal successors from generation to generation, even after the political charter rights were secured, the royal history thus impeached, and our people thus freed from royal control in many things, they were still forced, by the lack of other evidences, to submit to the royal control over our earliest history. And therefore this premeditated wrong of James I. has not been corrected. Even at the present day most of our histories of this movement (especially of the period prior to 1619), after altering some personal references to James I., would have been licensed for publication by his High Commission.

It will not be necessary to go to war in order to correct this wrong; for no one is any longer obliged either by law, by loyalty, or by an actual lack of other evidence to perpetuate the ideas of our national origin disseminated under the crown. There were formerly many reasons, from the political view of the Court party, why the royal government should support the utterly absurd ideas conveyed in the histories licensed by the crown of the grand movement for instituting the popular course of government in America; but there is no longer any reason, from the political view of the Patriot party, why we should continue to uphold the dishonorable work of James I. and his agents in these premises. To the contrary there is now every reason why our national government should be as anxious to reveal the true thews and sinews of our national origin, and to show that the plantations in America are a lasting monument to the popular course of government designed by Sir Edwin Sandys and our patriotic founders, and to preserve the evidences in proof thereof wheresoever they may be found, as the royal government was to conceal the fact; to destroy the evidences in proof thereof; and to produce the false impression that the plantations in America were a lasting monument to James I. and to the monarchical form of government designed by him.

Manifestly it was never just to rely upon the accounts published under the auspices of the royal government for our ideas of the beginning of the popular political reform movement conducted under the management of the Patriot party even when no other evidence was available; but (as I have outlined in Part III.) owing to circumstances formerly obtaining it has been, I may say, necessarily relied upon. The kings of England showed an ever-increasing determination to obliterate liberal political ideas; continued to exercise an especially absolute control over the freedom of the press and political matters in Virginia; and for many generations, with the exception of a brief period under the Commonwealth, when men's minds were completely occupied with the absorbing conditions then obtaining, the public had little or no option in the matter. The inspirations which shaped the ends of this movement were eliminated from the page of contemporary history; but these principles are immortal and could not be eliminated from the page of time.

When we consider the means adopted in the first instance, and the long control exercised over the evidences and the press by the advocates of the ideas of the Court party, we shall see that it is almost a miracle that any of the evidences favorable to the institution of a popular course of government in America escaped the determined efforts of the crown to have it all destroyed. But the truth conquers. The circumstances which formerly caused the publication of an inaccurate, incomplete account, and prevented the publication of a real history of this advance movement, have really been removed by the movement as it advanced. The Star Chamber and High Commission courts were removed under the advance of liberal ideas by the Parliament in 1641; the freedom of the press began under similar influence by special vote of the Commons in 1693; the standpoint of our political loyalty was revolutionized in 1776; and under Providence much of the evidence formerly confiscated and suppressed by the crown has been found by the laborers of the Republic in the field of original research looking for the truth. Although it may be that less than one fourth of the manuscript records of the original body politic have been found, yet included in these there is a great deal of very great public importance. A review of the case will show that since Beverley and Keith wrote their histories of Virginia nearly two centuries ago, the chief difficulties then in the way of rescuing the real history of our origin as a nation have been in a large measure removed, and we are at last able to have at least a fairly correct outline of "the most remarkable passages from the original to the dissolution of the Virginia Company."

The most important question now remaining is, not whether a great wrong was done our founders in the histories licensed under James I., for there can no longer be any question as to that fact; but the question is whether enough of the evidence confiscated by the king's commissioners has been found to enable us to correct the wrong. As to some periods enough has been found, as to others much is still missing; but as it is now our duty to consider all the evidence from the view point of the Patriot party, it will be found that much of the old evidence, in print and in manuscript, will convey different ideas from those formerly accepted, when thus considered. The particulars regarding which the evidence as yet found is insufficient, or entirely missing, are generally not of the greatest historical importance. There is certainly sufficient evidence now available to show the vital facts: that this nation had its origin in the greatest political reform movement of modern times; that James I. wished to stamp out the vital spark of this movement; that he determined for political reasons to obliterate all idea of its true character from history; that the history published under the auspices of the crown did this by depriving the enterprise of its inspiring features; and that save for the pious care of individuals every particle of our earliest political history — every vestige of the real inspiration of our national origin — would have been obliterated from the page of all history for all time.

An analysis of the evidences now available, with due reference to the point of view of the Patriot party, will show that past history has reversed the true view of this movement; that the historic sins are of omission as well as of commission, of a personal as well as of a public character; that inadequate ideas are given of the influence exerted on the movement by the various national parties of Church and State in England, and by the great continental powers — Spain, the Netherlands, and France; — and that entirely incorrect ideas are conveyed of the leading political features of the movement: of the charters under which the movement was conducted; of the corporation which conducted the movement; of the forms of government at issue; of the managers of the corporation, and of the motives which inspired them.

CHAPTER II

THE IDEA OF THE CHARTERS UNDER WHICH THE POLITICAL MOVEMENT WAS CONDUCTED, AS CONVEYED BY THE CROWN EVIDENCES, VERSUS THE CORRECT IDEA

In order to put a stop to (suppress) the institution of the popular course of government which the body politic, incorporated in the charters of 1609 and 1612, was inaugurating in this country, James I. determined to annul the popular charters. In order to justify this act and to obliterate the fact that the colony had been founded on the liberal idea of government to which his majesty was so much opposed, and not on the form designed by himself, the histories licensed under the crown do not show what the charter rights were, or what inspired the desire to obtain them, or who petitioned for them, or anything of any value about them — in fact, these historians really obliterated these charters from history so far as they could. The Rev. Samuel Purchas published an abstract of the royal charter of 1606; but the charters of 1609 and 1612 to the corporation were not published in, and a correct idea of them cannot be derived from, the contemporary histories, or from any history published prior to 1747. There is now enough evidence to show that these charters were the political foundation of the reform movement which was the beginning of our existence as a republic; and therefore it is of the first historic importance for us to understand them and all that pertains to them.

The charter of April, 1606, authorized a company, composed of adventurers only, "called the first colony," to settle a plantation of one hundred miles square along the Atlantic coast somewhere between 34° and 41° north latitude. This company was authorized to send out settlers at its own expense. But the company of adventurers and the settlers of the plantation were to be under officials appointed for them by and under a form of government designed for them by

James I.; they neither had the right to govern the proposed plantation, nor themselves — James I. took care of that. Even the ships sent by this company were under the charge of officers appointed by the colonial council of the king in England, commissioned under and responsible to the crown. This Virginia Company was not only not allowed to govern the plantation which was to be settled at its own expense; but the rights granted were limited, even the liberty of enjoying the rights of British subjects in the other dominions of the crown of Great Britain was confined by the patent to the settlers and their children. But as I have shown in Part I., both the North and South Virginia plantations failed under the administration of James I. The North and South Virginia companies were superseded by corporations and bodies politic under which both colonies were settled.

"A corporation and body politic," composed of both adventurers of the purse and planters of the country, "called The Treasurer and Company of Adventurers and Planters of the City of London for the first Colony in Virginia," was incorporated by the charter of June 2, 1609. And this charter "gave, granted, and confirmed" to the members of this body politic, their successors, and assigns forever, the whole boundary between 34° and 40° north latitude, extending from the Atlantic to the Pacific; "they paying to the crown the fifth part only of all ore of gold and silver that from time to time, and at all times hereafter, shall be there gotten."

Under the charters of 1609 and 1612 the body politic was authorized to add thereto new members, both adventurers of the purse and planters of the country, to an unlimited number; to secure and to settle this boundary; and to govern themselves and their dominion agreeably to the laws of England, "forever hereafter."

The grant of land conveyed by these charters embraced all or portions of the present New Jersey, Delaware, Pennsylvania, Maryland, District of Columbia, Virginia, West Virginia, North Carolina, South Carolina, Georgia, Alabama, Mississippi, Tennessee, Kentucky, Ohio, Indiana, Illinois, Missouri, Kansas, Arkansas, Indian Territory, Oklahoma, Texas, New Mexico, Colorado, Arizona, Utah, Nevada, and California.

The corporation not only had the especial political privilege of self-government in the dominion conveyed by these charters forever; but the planters, their children, and *their posterity* — the future citizens of that domain — were also to " enjoy all liberties, franchises and immunities *of free denizens and natural subjects,* within " any of the other dominions of the Crown of Great Britain, *forever.* Similar privileges were afterwards granted in North Virginia under the Massachusetts charter of 1629 and subsequent charters.

It is true that men inspired with liberal ideas were members of the company of 1606–1609, but they had no power to carry out those ideas under the charter of April, 1606. The definite beginning of the reform movement was with the petition for the charter incorporating a body politic in 1609. As soon as that petition was granted 'the worthy Patriots, Lords, Knights, gentlemen, merchants, and others made subscriptions to the amount of over $1,000,000 (present value) toward carrying forward the undertaking.' The charter granted in reply to this petition, under which the movement was to be inaugurated for taking the destiny of this country out of the column of Old World monarchies, and for instituting in America a popular course of government as a refuge from the absolute tyranny of the royal course of government in England, was signed on June 2, 1609 (N. S.), and was received at Jamestown on the first anniversary, June 2, 1610.

The reformation aimed at was of the utmost boldness, encroaching as it did on the royal prerogative — "the projected end" or object of the movement being the establishment of a more free government in the New World as a refuge from the absolute tyranny of the Old World. The means for altering the king's form of government and for the final accomplishment of the projected end were embodied in the charters of

1609 and 1612 by Sir Edwin Sandys. As he expressed it himself, he "purposed to erect a free popular State in Virginia," and was the "means of sending the charter into Virginia, in which is a clause that the people there shall have no government putt upon them but by their own consents."

The embryo of our popular course of government is found in these charters, and in the orders, commissions, instructions, constitutions, assemblies, and other political proceedings instituted under and authorized by these charters, which must be considered as the mother charters of our political system; and therefore whatever relates to them has a bearing on the subsequent politics and history of the whole country.

In carrying out the plan for setting up in America a government founded on civil and religious liberty, "the Pilgrims" sailed for South Virginia as members of our original body politic in 1620. The plantation of North Virginia under the charter of 1606 was to be under the administration of the crown, and the company incorporated under that charter could not have granted the Pilgrims the political right to form themselves into "a civill body politik" as they did do. The authority for the celebrated "Mayflower compact" was derived from Pierce's patent of February, 1620, granted by the Virginia Court under the authority derived from the charters of 1609 and 1612. And "the Pilgrims" were under no other authority until the arrival of the Fortune in November, 1621, with the official copy of the New England charter of November, 1620, and with "the first Plymouth patent" issued thereunder. And thus it was that the first actual settlement of both North and South Virginia was effected under the same charters, and under the influence of the same inspirations.[1]

Many members of the council named in the New England charter of November, 1620, were members of our original body politic. The charter was to "a body politic," but it was a limited and not a popular body, and was in accordance with the ideas of the Court party to which Sir F. Gorges and a majority of the council belonged, and in opposition to the wishes of the Patriot party in the Virginia Corporation. The issuing of this charter was in fact one of the first steps taken in the movement for annulling the popular charters of that corporation.[2]

Probably all of the twenty "Pattentees" under the Gorges charter, among whom New England was divided on July 9, 1623 (N. S.), were regarded as members of the Court party at that time. James I. himself drew the lots for

[1] See *The First Republic in America*, pp. 252, 262-266, 271-273, 283, etc.
[2] See *The First Republic in America*, pp. 361, 403, etc.

several of them. The Pilgrims who had settled in the country were not in accord with these men, nor in sympathy with their ideas. Upheld by their own religious purposes, they held on to the colony as best they could; but the vital political force was lacking, and in order to save the drooping colony, Charles I. in March, 1629, consented to grant to (North Virginia) Massachusetts the same political force which Sandys and the Patriots had called upon in 1609 and 1612 to save South Virginia. This charter was drafted by John White, an able advocate of our first political charter rights and a leading member of the primary body politic of this nation. This charter to "The Governor and Company [instead of "The Treasurer and Company"[1]] of the Mattachusetts Baye in Newe England" was modeled after the South Virginia charters of 1609 and 1612 and the proposed charter of 1621. It had to pass Lord Keeper Coventry, who as attorney-general had condemned the Virginia charter as "an unlimited vast patent," and the powers conveyed to "the one body politique and corporate" were not unlimited. But the political features were almost the same as those of the original popular charters, and evidently as broad as Charles I. would have granted, similar to those then being promised, and more liberal than he was then yielding to the South Virginia Colony.

[1] See *The First Republic in America*, p. 396.

The incorporators of the New England charter of November, 1620, surrendered their charter to the crown in 1635, and some of these men, members of the Court party, at once began to prosecute a suit in the Court of King's Bench for annulling the popular charter of the Massachusetts Corporation and body politic as they had formerly done against the original popular charters. But the people of Massachusetts managed to hold on to their popular charter for many years; like the people of Virginia, many of them, never really yielding their charter rights to the crown, finally secured them by force and arms. This Massachusetts charter, modeled after the original popular charters, came to supersede to a large extent the royal charter of 1620, and became virtually the direct basis for the subsequent North Virginia charters. Thus the popular charter rights of both North and South Virginians were derived from the same originals, were very similar, and it is equally the patriotic duty of both North and South Virginians to protect the true history of those originals from the determination of James I. and the Court party to obliterate it.

When "The First Republic in America," written with the intention of aiding in the correction of this historic wrong, was published in 1898, the advocates of the crown evidences called up the influence of present sectional politics to aid them in perpetuating the wrong committed under the influence of past imperial politics. On the one side Northern readers were told, "We will have to look further north for the first republic in America," etc., and on the other, Southern readers were assured that I was writing under Northern training, influence, etc.

I do not wish to be understood as denying any of the honors due the founders of any portion of our country or of any period of our national existence, for this is not my intention. Everything has a beginning. I am trying to give the correct idea of the charters of 1609 and 1612; to show the political importance of these charters, from which was first derived the authority to inaugurate in America the popular political principles on which our country was founded, and to prove that so far from the question of our earliest history being one of a sectional character it is one of mutual interest and importance to both sections of our country. It is with this object that I call attention to the facts — that New England was first settled under those charters and afterwards perpetuated under a charter based on them, and that Charles I. for similar reasons yielded to the Massachusetts Corporation similar political rights to those which James I. had formerly yielded to the Virginia Corporation. Charles I. did not commit the historic wrong of having the charter of the Massachusetts body politic annulled, records confiscated, and history published; but North Virginians are really as much interested in correcting the wrong done by James I. as South Virginians are, yet sectional opinions seem to be the greatest obstacles now in the way of the correction of the wrong. It is essential to show that these influences cannot be fairly called upon in this matter. The patriotic citizens of North and of South Virginia were certainly equally interested in securing the charter rights of which James I. and his successors wished to deprive our forefathers; and by the same token North and South Virginians are equally interested in securing the historic honors of which James I. did deprive our patriotic founders. Our founders, at the expense of their blood and treasure, first settled this country upon popular political charter rights. The crown, wishing to deprive them of those rights, suppressed the facts, compiled documents, and licensed histories to justify the act. Our forefathers, at the expense of their blood and treasure, finally secured those rights to this country, and there is no reason why any citizen of this republic should follow evidences written to prove that those rights ought not to have been granted in the first place and ought to have been annulled by the crown. It is not possible to make a sectional matter of this historic question. The patriotic citizens of North Virginia, and of every portion of the United States who appreciate the value of popular political principles of government, are as much obliged to protect the true history of the primal institution of those principles in our country from the effects of the original historic wrong as the citizens of South Virginia. The wrong was committed under the auspices of the national government of England. North Virginian historians have probably done as much as those of South Virginia towards perpetuating it. The duty of correcting the wrong is a national one; it falls alike on every citizen of the republic to venerate and protect everything relative to our patriotic founders.

The eyes of all Europe [1] had been looking upon the endeavors of the patriotic managers of the Virginia enterprise to plant an English nation in America for many years, and when the Old World saw that the popular American idea of our patriotic founders, "inviting people to withdraw themselves from an oppressing into a more free government establishing in Virginia," was inspiring the English plantation with vitality, in the face of great obstacles, where there had been only failure before, companies or corporations with similar aspirations were chartered in England, Holland,[2] and other nations, with political as well as commercial privileges; and the inspi-

---

[1] See *The Genesis of the United States*, vol. i. p. 463.
[2] See *The First Republic in America*, pp. 450, 492.

ration spread until it covered the American Continent. It is still spreading. Our popular political system has not only kept freedom alive in the New World, but has reinvigorated it in the Old World. 'The ideas flowing through the young blood of American Liberty have been transfused into some of the aged systems of European polity, and by a more healthful and generous circulation has restored them in a degree to youth, activity, and strength.'

CHAPTER III

THE CHARACTER OF THE CORPORATION WHICH CONDUCTED THE POLITICAL MOVEMENT AS REPRESENTED IN THE CROWN EVIDENCES, AND AS IT REALLY WAS

In order to give a correct idea of the charters, I have in the previous chapter given a general idea of the companies incorporated by them; but I wish to give a more detailed account of the Virginia companies. The importance of the enterprise from the first cannot be denied; but the Virginia Company, to which certain privileges were granted in the charter of 1606, cannot be considered as a free political agent in such a matter as the beginning of a nation, for it was entirely under the government of James I. Whatever was accomplished under this company would naturally be attributed by the Court party ("the powers that be") to the wisdom and genius of the king through his representatives, who were the managers of the government; while all blame would be laid on the company officials, who were the managers of the business. And under the political influence of these circumstances the history licensed by the crown is devoted to giving an overshadowing prominence to what was done under the king's administration; while it omits or belittles or criticises nearly everything done, not only by the managers of the business during 1606–1609, but also by the political corporation which really laid the foundation of the nation during 1610–1624. James I. wished to rob the political movement of all honors, and the licensed history not only omitted the popular charters, but an entirely incorrect idea is conveyed of the body politic incorporated by them. It is necessary to have a correct idea of the character of this political corporation in order to understand the case of our founders; and among the numerous confused and false impressions produced of this political body by the crown evidences it is especially important to correct the following ideas frequently found in histories: That "The Virginia Court," which met in London from 1612 to 1624, was "The Virginia Company;" that "the colony in Virginia was the property of a Company in London;" that "the colony in

Virginia was ruled by a Company in London;" and that this "Company in London" was "an ordinary joint-stock company," "a strictly commercial company," "a company for trade," "a company of merchants," "the proprietor of Virginia in the same sense that Lord Baltimore was the proprietor of Maryland," etc.

It is true that the enterprise was carried on at the expense of a company of adventurers while it was under the king's government (1606–1609), which hoped to be reimbursed by finding gold, a ready way to the South Sea, or other present profit. But after 1609 the movement was carried on by a "corporation and body politic," composed of both adventurers of the purse and planters of the country, having other aspirations and inspirations besides those of trade and personal profit, incorporated at a time when it was really known that the Indians of Virginia had "little to trade for but dried mulberryes;" at a time when the dangerous character of the climate and of the Indians of Virginia had been found out, as well as the numerous difficulties, at home and abroad, by land and by sea, which would have to be met and overcome at the expense of the corporation. It is true that the expense of conducting the movement was borne entirely under the joint-stock system for the first seven years (1609–1616) and partly so afterwards. But the object of this was not ordinary trade; the plan was adopted in order to enable the body politic to secure their country at the expense of the corporation without aid from the crown. The real stock was not stock in trade, but stock in a new dominion in which they could govern themselves. It is true that after a good many years the corporation was so fortunate as to find in tobacco a paying Virginia commodity; but, as Gondomar well said, there were farther designs than the making of a tobacco plantation.

It is true that Sir Thomas Smith was interested in, and was a leading advocate in Parliament of, the trading companies; was a protectionist, and came to be regarded as a monopolist by some members of the Virginia courts; but it is equally true that Sir Edwin Sandys, the leader in the political features of the movement, was bitterly opposed to these trusts, and was an earnest advocate of free trade. Both protectionists and free-traders had each been opposed by the Court party in some respects, and each of these men had been elected to preside over the supreme court of our original body politic, not because of their opinions regarding trade, but because they were regarded politically as Patriots; and when Smith's patriotism came to be questioned he found it agreeable to withdraw.

It seems well to explain here that there were many trust companies at that time, and the Virginia Corporation has sometimes been confused with them and described as "a syndicate or trust." It is true that some members of the trusts were also members of this company; but it was opposite to a trust, it was really an unlimited popular body in which the leaders of its political features were the leading opponents of these trusts. When the list of monopolies (which were being protested against by the Patriot party) was read in Parliament, William Hakewell, of this Virginia Corporation, called out to know if "bread were among them." Early in 1610 Hakewell maintained "The Liberty of the subject," in an able argument before Parliament, which, owing to the censorship of the press, was not published until after 1641.

The corporate or corporation system administered on a popular plan was the seed of the American idea of government. The charters of 1609 and 1612 were granted to an incorporation, composing a political body of planters of the country and adventurers of the purse, organized for the purpose of acquiring the lands of South Virginia at their own expense, and of instituting therein a government — "on the consent of the people, by the people, for the people" — in accord with the constitutions of England, but as interpreted in the most beneficial manner for the body politic, which was destined to become the people — the citizens — of that territory.

As soon as the members of this body began

the institution of their popular political plans in that territory, "the popularnes of the government of the corporation became displeasing to his Majesty;" he determined to annul the political charters in order to make the corporation "a company for trade, but not for government of the country," and to take care of the government himself.

It is true that some members of the corporation, who were unwilling to contend with James I. about the government, were willing to give up their political and property charter rights, and to allow the political corporation to be superseded by a trading company according to the desire of the crown, and that it was sometimes called by contemporaries, "A Company of English merchants trading to Virginia;" but as Strype well says, "the trading company was never incorporated." The political principles, the right of the people "for government of the Country," were never entirely superseded by the crown; and regardless of the desires of the Court party as expressed in the history licensed by the crown, and in other evidences of the crown, the fact remains that the organization which founded the first English colony in our country was a company in the sense of "a corporation and body politic" (composed of adventurers of the purse, planters of the country, and their successors forever, not restricted in numbers and only partially so as to nationality[1]). And this popular political body was the proprietor of South Virginia in very nearly the same sense that a similar body afterwards became the proprietor of North Virginia, and that our national corporation and body politic is now the proprietor of this country.

At the Virginia Court in London held on June 19, 1619, the auditors of the corporation, who had been "digesting of the old accounts" down to the end of the first joint stock (December 10, 1616), were required to extend their work to May 8, 1619. The task was found to be very difficult, and the Virginia Court of December 25, 1619, in order to expedite the auditing, determined to publish the names of every adventurer, with their several sums adventured, and appointed Sir Edwin Sandys and Dr. Thomas Winstone to draft the said publication. The following auditors were, from first to last, employed in compiling and verifying this list: Sir Edwin Sandys, Sir John Danvers, Mr. John Wroth, Mr. John Ferrar, Mr. Thomas Keightley, Mr. Henry Briggs, Mr. William Cranmer, Mr. William Essington, Mr. Richard Wiseman, Mr. George Chambers, Mr. Morris Abbott, Mr. Humphrey Handford, and Mr. Anthony Abdy. Both the Sandys and Smythe parties in the company were represented. A license was granted on July 21, 1620, and the list was published, "that Pos-

[1] See *The Charter of 1612*, Arts. I., X., XI., etc.

teritie may truely know by whose charges this Plantation hath beene happily founded, maintained, and continued." In case any one had not received his due credit, " if within one twelve moneth after the date hereof he give notice and make proof thereof to the Companies Auditors, he shall be set right,[1] and the Table reformed : there being not anything more dear unto us than to do right unto them with all justifiable curtesie, who have beene beginners and continuers of this glorious work," etc.

The value of this list with the sums paid by each cannot be overestimated, for it really does enable " posteritie to know truely " whose " treasure " had founded, maintained, and continued the plantation up to December 10, 1616, and in part to May, 1619. The sums did not include the amounts paid by private planters after 1616, nor the amounts received from the lotteries since 1612, for which they thanked, or pretended to thank, James I., although " he never contributed one farthing himself in them." The complete list contains nearly nine hundred adventurers who had adventured about $1,000,000, at present values.

In his books Captain John Smith virtually claims to having founded, maintained, and continued the plantation pretty much by himself,

[1] I have made use of this list as corrected in the biographies given in *The Genesis of the United States*, pp. 810-1067.

for several years, at an expense of more than five hundred pounds of his own estate, etc. In this list he is credited with having paid only nine pounds. Before the year of grace allowed claimants had expired, Captain Smith appeared before the Virginia Court (May 12, 1621) and put in a claim, not on the ground that Sir Thomas Smith had failed to give him credit for over four hundred and ninety-one pounds, but for services which, "as he allegeth," he had performed in Virginia. The opponents of Sir Thomas Smith, who were then controlling the business and searching for evidences against Sir Thomas in these very premises, would have been very willing to allow this claim (as they did allow the claims of others) if at all just; but the petition was referred to the committees appointed for the rewarding of men upon merits, and they allowed Captain Smith nothing.

This list is the only one of the numerous publications of the managers which contains the name of Captain John Smith; and the only reference to him that I have found in the records of the Virginia courts in London is in connection with the aforesaid petition of May, 1621. The only reference to him that I have found in the records of the courts held in Virginia, so far as they have been preserved, is in the deposition of Robert Poole and Edward Grindon on November 11, 1624, to the effect that he was the first Englishman to teach the Indians the use of firearms. In his books he charges Yeardley and other officers of the corporation with having done this. In brief, save for the evidences of the crown or crown evidences, — and especially those contributed by himself, — the historian licensed under the crown would be almost an unknown quantity in our earliest history.

The alphabetical list of adventurers published by the managers in 1620 was reprinted in Smith's history in 1624, but the reprint was not complete: it conveys no idea of the importance of the original, the amounts paid in by each person being *omitted*. And as a further illustration of the historian's mode of compiling, it will be noted that the name of his old patron, "Edward Semer Earle of Hartford," who was not an adventurer, had contributed nothing to the enterprise, was inserted.

It must be remembered that this published list only pretends to give the adventurers of the purse. It is not a complete list of the body politic at that time. The planters who went over in person, paying their own way, and those sent over at the expense of the corporation fund (after they had served out their time in repayment of the advance), became freemen, citizens, voters, and members of the political body. A complete record of the planters and of those sent over was kept; but as it was among the records confiscated by the crown, and as no complete copy has been found, many of their names have been unfortunately lost.

As the movement in the beginning was carried on largely at the expense of the adventurers of the purse, their position may be considered as at first of the greatest importance, especially as those who paid in as much as £12.10 — say $300 now — were also landowners in the colony. But as the movement progressed under the proposed system, as the country became more securely settled, and after a proper form of government was instituted therein, the planters increasing more and more would naturally become the majority and control the country; but there was nothing to prevent the adventurers, or their heirs, from coming over and settling on their lands in the country themselves. Many of them did so, and this was probably the ultimate object of most of them, as indicated in Coventry's speech in the *Quo Warranto* case in June, 1624.

The motive of the patriotic members (both adventurers and planters) of the corporation was really the same. In order to secure their political and property charter rights, the "adventurer" contributed his "treasure," and the "planter" devoted his life "blood." Some of the adventurers of the purse through discontent, through opposition to the advance political purposes of the Patriots when they became known, or other cause, refused to pay their dues; and some of the planters deserted the colony, and thus ceased to be members of the body politic. Of the adventurers who remained members, some of them, or their heirs, came over, settled on their lands, and became planters; some sold their lands to others who became planters; and others had their estates in Virginia managed for them by planters. All of those who complied with the requirements of the corporation, both adventurers and planters, they and their posterity and successors, were equally members of the political body (citizens of Virginia), and heirs to the political privileges and charter rights forever.

The colony under the proposed system, although attached to the crown of Great Britain, naturally drifted farther and farther away from the crown. The Court party controlled the evidences, and the acts of the Patriot party were kept almost out of sight in our annals; but when the proper time came for our independence, although Tories were still governing in the colonies, the Patriots were found to be sufficiently strong to secure it.

Jefferson was correct when he said that "the ball of the Revolution received its first impulse, not from the actors in that event, but from the first colonists." The Virginia companies of 1606 were superseded by corporations and bodies politic which secured and founded the first

English colonies in the present United States, — under their own management, at the expense of their own blood and treasure, on their popular political principles of government, unassisted by the crown, and regardless of the opposition of the Court party. The records of the primary body politic were confiscated by the crown, false ideas of that body were conveyed in the history licensed under the crown and perpetuated both under the crown and under the Republic; but the fact remains that the foundation of this nation was laid upon the immortal principles which are still giving it vitality, and that the heart of the political body which planted the germ of the popular course of government in our country has never ceased to beat.

CHAPTER IV

THE FORMS OF GOVERNMENT AT ISSUE — THE FORM DESIGNED FOR THE AMERICAN PLANTATIONS BY JAMES I., WHICH WAS ADVOCATED BY THE COURT PARTY, *vs.* THE FORM DESIGNED FOR THEIR SOUTH VIRGINIAN TERRITORY BY THE CORPORATION AND BODY POLITIC, WHICH WAS ADVOCATED BY THE PATRIOT PARTY

The Court party and the historian licensed by the crown contended that the colony of Virginia was founded under a form of government designed by James I., and that the great reform movement for inaugurating the popular course of government in this country resulted in failure. But there is now sufficient evidence to show that the ideas conveyed by the crown evidences as to the opposing forms of government and as to their effect on the plantations are not correct. As a matter of fact it was the king's form of government, of which the historian was a representative, that failed. And it was the popular course of government, to which the historian was opposed, that lighted the lamp of liberty and kindled the fires of political independence in this country which have never failed.

Rev. Mr. Stith[1] published for the first time an outline of the king's form under which the South Virginia plantation was governed from 1607 to 1610. This outline, compiled from the notes of Sir John Randolph, is as follows: "I shall only transiently remark," says Stith, "that notwithstanding the frequent Repetition of the Laws of England and the Equity thereof, his Majesty seems, in some things, to have deviated grossly from them. He has certainly made sufficient Provision for his own despotic Authority; and has attributed [conferred] an extravagant and illegal Power to the Presidents and Councils. For he has placed the whole Legislative Power

[1] See his *History of Virginia* (1747), p. 41.

solely in them, without any Representative of the People, contrary to a noted Maxim of the English Constitution; That all Freemen are to be governed by Laws, made with their own consent, either in Person, or by their Representatives. He has also appointed Juries only in Cases of Life and Death; and has left all other Points, relating to the Liberty and private Property of the subject, wholly to the Pleasure and Determination of the Presidents and Councils," etc. Mr. Stith failed to note the important fact that the colony was not only under the king's form of government, but also under the king's officials. "*The Presidents and Councils*" were "all nominated by his Majesty," appointed under and responsible to the crown. They were the *king's representatives, not the company's*, in Virginia. This company had not the right of self-government.

Although the body politic of 1609 had obtained the privilege of "governing themselves," there was need for discretion in proceeding with their plans. The charters were so designed and the authority derived from them so executed, as not to create suspicion by causing the king's absolute authority over the enterprise to pass from him immediately but gradually, until in due time the political body would be enabled to establish a popular course of government in Virginia in which the people, the planters, should have an independent political power. In England the members of the first king's council for the corporation were appointed by James I. in the charter of 1609, but subsequent members were to be "freely" elected by the Corporation; and thus in a few years the supreme authority of the movement really passed into the Quarter Court of the Virginia Corporation, which came to be regarded as "a Seminary of Sedition" by the crown.

In Virginia the government was for sufficient reason at first placed by the supreme council in England (which had first been appointed by James I.) in charge of an absolute governor, who appointed his own council in the colony; but this also changed as the movement advanced, until the governor and his council in Virginia were "freely elected" by the majority of the votes cast by the adventurers and planters (the landowners in Virginia) in the General Quarterly Courts then held in London. Thus they were the officials not of the crown, but of the Virginian Corporation, being elected by and responsible to that body; and a House of Burgesses was freely elected by the votes of all the men on the different "Burgs" in Virginia, whether they owned land or not, this body being the chosen representative of the planters — the people of Virginia.

This issue was probably the chief cause of the commission of the original wrong by James I., and therefore it is very important to understand clearly this portion of the controversy. I wish to make the case as clear as I can.

Under the charter of 1606 the government of the companies and plantations was under officials appointed under the crown, amenable to the crown, and under a form of government designed by James I.

In order to alter this form of government and for other reasons already given, the charter of 1609 was obtained, under which the officials were first appointed by James I., but were afterwards elected by the majority of the company. See Articles IX., XI., XIII., XIV., and XXIII.

In order to still further "better the government of the company and the colony," etc., the charter of 1612 was obtained, under which the Great and General Quarter Courts (composed of members both of the council and of the generality) of the corporation had a general supervision over the government of the colony.[1] The acts of the Assembly in Virginia were at first subject to review by these supreme courts, for in the beginning all things were in a formative state; but "after the colony was well framed and settled, no order of the Quarter Court was to be binding on the colony until it was ratified by the General Assembly in Virginia," and no taxes, revenues, etc., were to be imposed on the

[1] Article VIII.

colonists "other ways than by the authority of the said Assembly." London and Virginia were in the same empire. The Virginia Corporation had interests in London as well as in Virginia, and these supreme courts were held in London; but, as was afterwards the case in the Massachusetts charter, there was nothing in the Virginia charter of 1612 to prevent the removal of these courts to Virginia whenever it became to the interest of the colony to do so. And the first thing that James I. did after the charters were annulled was to suppress these courts.

James I. was really bitterly opposed to the popular course of government which the Virginia Corporation was inaugurating in this country, and had evidently granted the political privileges to that corporation (to pull the chestnut out of the fire) in order to have the colonies secured and founded without any expense to the crown; for as soon as the country was thus secured, he determined to annul the popular charters, to make the body politic "a company for trade, but not for government of the country" — which was the business of kings and not of people — and to resume the government of the country himself.

Although the Virginia courts which had met in England were suppressed by the crown, and in lieu thereof the colonial affairs were managed in England by royal commissioners, plantation boards, etc., from 1624 to 1776 — under Providence the body politic (generally called in history " The Virginia Company of London ") was never really destroyed; the members thereof in the colony — the citizens of Virginia — were allowed by the crown to retain some of their political charter rights, freedoms, and privileges, and they never ceased to claim the rest. They had tasted the sweets of self-government, a flavor once tasted never to be forgotten. The petitions presented to the crown from time to time, from 1624 to 1774, by the Patriot party of Virginia, were for the restitution of their popular charters; for the colonial affairs to be again managed by courts of the corporation, instead of by royal commissions, etc.; or for some special political or property charter right of which they had been deprived by the crown. Of course, there was no need to petition for the restitution of " a Proprietary Company," or for any other kind of company which had never existed in the premises; nor for any charter right which had not been taken away; but the Royalist party, to offset the petitions of the Patriots sometimes sent in counter petitions, in which they present the issues from the political point of view of the Court party, which, it can now be proven, was always misleading and unjust to the Patriot party.

No government was ever instituted in which the political principles of a government of the people, for the people, by the people were carried farther than in the representative or popular course of government which was inaugurated in this country by the founders of South Virginia on the political rights derived by them from the charters of 1609 and 1612. Every "burg" or corporation was represented by one of its people in the House of Burgesses from 1619 to 1634, when the colony was first divided into shires or counties. The right of suffrage exercised by all freemen was not restricted until the Assembly of March, 1655, limited suffrage to "all housekeepers, freeholders, leaseholders, or tenants;" but the next Assembly of March, 1656, "thinking it somewhat hard and unagreeable to reason that any persons shall pay taxes and have no votes in election," restored universal suffrage, with the *proviso* that the votes were to be given by ballot (the original — 1619–1646 — plan) instead of *viva voce* as had been the law from 1647 to 1655. The first effectual restriction of suffrage was under Charles II. from 1670 to 1676, to freeholders and housekeepers. The restrictive clause was revoked by Bacon's Assembly in June, 1676, and universal suffrage prevailed during 1676–1684; suffrage again restricted to freeholders and housekeepers from 1684 to 1699; and in 1699 to "none but freeholders;" but this restriction was almost only in name, as the owner of so little as half an acre was regarded as a freeholder until 1736, when definite restriction began; but the spirit of liberty in the hearts of the people was never restricted. The summer session of the House of Burgesses in 1748 promised to be almost as incorrigible as Bacon's Assembly in 1676, but the royal governor prorogued the body and afterwards dissolved it and ordered a new election. The plan having met with success, the dissolving of the House of Burgesses became more and more frequent with the royal governors until it aided in bringing on the Revolution which dissolved our connection with the royal government.

In brief, sufficient evidence for the Patriot party has been providentially preserved to prove that "the plantations in America" do not remain as a lasting monument to the imperial form of government designed for them by James I., but that they do remain as a lasting monument to the popular course of government inaugurated in them by our Patriot founders.

CHAPTER V

THE CHARACTER OF "THE MANAGERS OF THE BUSINESS" IN ENGLAND AND IN VIRGINIA, AND OTHER ISSUES OF A POLITICAL NATURE

THE Virginia Company of 1606-1609 conducted the colonial business affairs at its own expense; but the political management was under James I. And there was a natural clash between the managers of the business for the company, and the royal officials who managed the government for the crown. Hence imperial politics had as bad an effect on the royal accounts of the managers of the business before the enterprise became a reform movement as after. Much of the history licensed under the crown is really an adverse criticism of the managers of the business — of those who paid the expenses, and of those who went to Virginia — from 1606 to 1624; an effort to show their incapacity, lack of judgment, and "misgovernment," as opposed to the great capacity and genius of the historian who had been the loyal representative of James I. There is little if any evidence to prove the capacity of this historian that is certainly fair and free from his own dictation; but there is ample evidence to show that the leading managers were the most progressive men in one of the most remarkable transition periods in English history, and that they were showing good judgment by adopting the principles of liberty which have sustained this nation from its birth, which the Court party and the historian considered as "misgovernment."

Sir Thomas Smith and other leading managers of the corporation for the period of 1609–1618 afterwards affiliated with the Court party, and not only made no effort to preserve copies of the records of their own administration, but actually aided the crown in suppressing them. And while the managers of 1619-1624 made earnest efforts to preserve their own evidence, they regarded the old managers as then being their adversaries, and were, also, actually disposed to aid the Court party by finding fault with the management during that period — not only by Sir Thomas Smith in England, but also by Dale, Gates, and others in Virginia. And this evidence has been taken as corroborative of the royal evidences, but the motive for this evidence is self-evident. And even if there were no other counter evidence, the speech of Sir Edward Sandys himself on November 27, 1619, in praise of the services of Gates and Dale, would be sufficient.

It may also be noted that when John Smith, of Nibley, in April, 1621, proposed to the Virginia Court 'to have a fair and perspicuous history compiled of Virginia,' one of his especial objects was to 'transmit to all posterity the memory and fame of Sir Thomas Dale, the Lord De la Warr, and Sir Thomas Gates,' — three men who had been chief managers of the business in Virginia for nearly the whole of the important crucial period from May, 1610, to April, 1616. As a result of these party controversies and political conditions, the authentic evidences for the period of 1609–1618 are especially incomplete, and therefore it is not possible to correct in every detail the historic wrong done the managers during this period; but we now know that it was in many respects the most important period in our history. It was in this period that our first political charter rights were obtained; that the most serious difficulties in Virginia and with Spain were to a large degree overcome; that the actual hold on the country was secured, popular rights inaugurated, and political life began.

The crown evidences are unjust to the managers of the business for the whole period from 1606 to 1624; this wrong has been partially corrected, however, in our histories by Stith and others for 1619–1624; but beginning with the historian licensed by the crown and following him as an authority and as a model, some of our historians have almost vied with each other in an ungenerous, unjust, and incorrect treatment of the managers of this movement during 1606–1618, and especially during the important period, 1609–1618. The intention of the licensed historian in doing this was to produce the impression that the alteration from the king's management to that of the corporation was for the worse. And in sustaining this historian, subsequent historians have been equally unjust to the managers; they have blamed them for placing the colony under martial law; for not settling emigrants at once

on lands of their own, etc., — regardless of the
fact that it would evidently have been folly to
attempt a settled government and to settle definite bounds of lands before the country itself
was practically secured from the Spaniards or
the Indians. The conditions were such that for
a good many years martial law was necessary.
In fact a settled government and land grants
were instituted as soon as it was practicable and
advisable.

The accounts of the planters who went, and of
the emigrants who were sent to Virginia, given
in the crown evidences, are very unfavorable to
them; but it is evident that they were a representative body composed of all sorts of people,
from the lowest to the highest, and that the
worst were those sent over by order of the
crown.

The political point of view has as much to do
with the biography of the men engaged in the
colonial movement as with the history of the
movement. The same man might be considered
a rebel by one party and a Patriot by the other;
an impostor by one party and a hero by the
other; a convict under the crown might be a
martyr to liberty. Let me give a single example.

The evidences written from the political point
of view of the Court party are especially severe
on Captain John Radcliffe, but it is now known

that he was chosen to command the Discovery in the first fleet sent to the colony by the company under the crown, and brought that cockleshell safely across the Atlantic with planters and supplies to Virginia in 1606–1607; that he was appointed under James I. to his council in Virginia; that as president of that council he governed the colony from September, 1607, to September, 1608, under the form of government designed for the plantations by James I., saw its defects, was man enough to protest against them, and was instrumental in obtaining the new charter under which "the popular course" of government was inaugurated; that he was selected to command the vice-admiral ship in the first fleet sent under the body politic in 1609, and brought that ship over the Atlantic through the great tempest to Virginia with planters and supplies; that Captain George Percy gave him credit for the part taken by him in suppressing the effort of Captain John Smith to set up "A Soveraigne Rule" in Virginia, and that by the treachery of Powhatan his life was taken while he was actively engaged in carrying forward the colonial enterprise in Virginia. He gave his own blood and about $1000 (present value) of his own treasure toward securing this country for us, and is one of the martyrs of our genesis. From the patriotic view point he deserves much more consideration from the historians of this

Republic than he would have done if he had brought nothing to Virginia, had landed here himself restrained as a prisoner, had been sent back to England to answer for some misdemeanors, had not returned to Virginia, had not given his life to the great cause, but had devoted himself to writing "histories" lauding himself, criticising our patriotic founders, conforming with the purposes of the crown, and opposing the principles on which our country was founded. And if the original history of the enterprise had been written from the view point of the Patriot party, he would have been lauded therein as one of the founders of Virginia — as a Virginian hero — instead of being abused, as has been done in our histories based on the evidences of the Court party.

Nothing is of greater historic importance than a proper political classification and analysis of our colonial evidences. In order to secure colonies without using the royal revenues, the kings of England granted charters to corporations and bodies politic conveying to them not only commercial but political privileges. In order to secure these charter rights, these bodies settled their grants at the expense of their own blood and treasure, unaided by the crown. After the colonies were thus secured, the crown annulled their charters and attempted to suppress their history. The dominions settled by them on popular rights were domineered over by, and the histories of their acts were published under the auspices of, royal officials. But the citizens of the country knew the great value to them of the political principles which the Court party (the crown) was trying to take from them, and which they had settled in this country to secure. Therefore these popular charter rights remained a constant ground of contention from 1610 to 1776, and there were always two parties in the colony contending over these rights — a popular element and a Royalist or Tory element. In Virginia the evidences were largely under the control of the crown officials, the leaders of the Royal party, and only traces of evidences favorable to the Patriot party have escaped destruction in the public record offices in England and in Virginia. This is especially true of the foundation period, 1606-1625, and of such periods as 1630-1635, 1640-1660, 1674-1677, etc.; but probably of no period while Virginia was under the crown has there been preserved sufficient authentic and reliable evidence upon which to base complete and absolutely accurate historical narrative of events. And probably the greater part of her colonial history has been based on the *ex parte* evidences for the crown. After giving due consideration to the evidences that remain and to the circumstances which inspired them and controlled them, I feel sure that the popular element was always very strong in Virginia. And evidences preserved by the crown to the contrary notwithstanding, the crown was always well aware of this fact, as the constant effort of royal officials to obliterate evidences and of royal writers to produce the contrary impression amply proves. I feel sure that the emigrants to Virginia came over as much for the sake of more freedom of thought and action as for anything else; and that this was not only true in business and politics, but also in religion. The broad-minded member of the Church of England wished to exercise a freedom of thought and of action, as much so as the Non-conformists of England, the Huguenots of France, the Presbyterians of the north of Ireland, and the Episcopalians of Scotland. Many from each of these classes certainly came to Virginia. Whether they came to escape the rule of an absolute monarchy when that power was ruling Great Britain, or to escape the Roundheads of 1646–1659, or for whatever reason they came, a large majority of all became advocates of the popular political charter rights upon which the colony was founded, rather than of the royal rule which they had left behind them in the Old World. And when the time that tried men's souls came, Patriots were not found wanting in Virginia.

CHAPTER VI

VIS VITÆ — THE MOTIVE OF THE MOVEMENT AS IT WAS REPRESENTED IN THE EVIDENCES FROM THE VIEW POINT OF THE COURT AND PATRIOT PARTIES

OF all things James I. was evidently most determined to efface every trace of the vital force which really sustained this movement from the first, through almost insurmountable difficulties.

The idea conveyed by the crown history is that the managers of the business in sending out the colony were inspired by an inordinate desire for gain; but as usual with the crown evidences this was as opposite to the truth as the Court party was opposed to the purposes of the Patriots. In accordance with the universal harmony of things, everything in nature must be produced by a special germ, — a prime principle sustaining vitality, — and it was the inspiring desire to escape tyranny and to find freedom, which gave the touch of life to the English-American colonies, and which continues to sustain the vitality of this nation.

Prior to 1609 the idea had been, as expressed by Lane to Raleigh, that "the discovery of a gold mine by the goodness of God, or a passage to the South Sea, or some way to it, and nothing else, can bring America in request to be inhabited by our Nation." After repeated trials no route to the South Sea was found, and the gold found by the Spaniards in South America was not found by the English in North America; but it so happened that " the free air " of Virginia, acting as an inspiration on the minds of some of the first planters, was instrumental in producing in the enlarged minds of the men of genius who were then adopting the principles of liberty the determination to put those political principles in practice in America, and it was this " projected end," more than anything else, which brought this country in request to be inhabited by our nation.

It was not for the sake of gain, but for the sake of the special privileges, immunities, and liberal charter rights that our primary body politic undertook to settle this country at the expense of their own blood and treasure. Human beings cannot meet and overcome constant, long continued expense and disaster without any recompense unless they are sustained by a " Divine Agency, working through Special Providence." The love of liberty is a divine principle placed in every human heart by God, and it was the inspired spirit of liberty which enabled the patriotic managers of the movement to overcome the results of past misgovernment and disappointment and to continue their enterprise in the face of the bitter opposition of Spain and the increasing unfriendliness of the Court party; meeting as well as human beings could do the dangers and difficulties, known and unknown, of the new lands and seas,—"lightning and tempest, plague, pestilence, and famine, battle and murder and sudden death;" going to great expense without any reward, with a constant resolution, until, "by the mercy of God," they succeeded in laying the foundation for a new nation in the new world on popular political principles for the betterment of their posterity and for the advancement of mankind.

As I have shown in my previous books, the chief avowed objects of the Virginia Corporation prior to 1618 had been their intention of spreading the commonwealth, the commerce, and the Church of England; but it is now certain that the political purpose, although not avowed, had really been the inspiration, the soul, of the movement since 1609; and that the patriotic members of the body politic—both planters and adventurers—had constantly looked forward to the institution of the proposed popular political principles.

And throughout the whole movement the hand of a divine agency can be seen working through special providences. It was providential that the plantations of 1607, in North and in South

Virginia, failed under the political control of James I. It was providential that the special charters to the original of the body politic of this nation were granted. It was providential that the plan of government designed for the plantations in North and South Virginia by James I. was altered. It was providential that James I. died when he did, and that Charles I. was under peculiar personal obligations to some of the Patriots in the Virginia corporation. It was providential that the issue between the Crown and the Commons was a protection to the popular purposes of the corporation from 1609 to 1659, thus enabling the growing tree of liberty to become sufficiently deep-rooted in America to withstand successfully the opposition of the crown as it increased after 1660. In brief, it was providential that the popular course of government was instituted in both North and South Virginia, and that the actual foundation of this country was laid under the political management of men inspired with liberal ideas of government; for the prosecution of the plantations to the political purposes which were especially condemned by James I., the Court party, and the historians licensed under the crown was really the inspiration, — *vis vitæ*, — the soul of the movement, under which our country was secured for us, and made the seat of liberty, enlightenment, and good government in the New World. To translate the figurate language of the first great seal of the State of Virginia, it was 'In this way that God made us Free! Thus Virtue overcame Tyranny!'

CHAPTER VII

CONCLUSION — A SUMMARY OF THE CASE OR CONTROVERSY

THE question as to whether Pocahontas rescued Captain John Smith from the clubs of the savages of King Powhatan is not of so great historic importance, and I have never so considered it. The important question has been whether the true history of our beginning as a nation could be rescued from the acts of the agents of King James I. Notwithstanding all difficulties, the obstacles formerly in the way have been sufficiently removed to enable us to have at least a fair idea of the importance of the case.

The Patriot party managed the business and laid the foundation upon which this great nation has been erected. The Court party controlled the evidences and laid the foundation upon which the history of this movement has been written. The value of the services of those two great parties in their respective fields must be judged by the results which have followed the acceptation of their respective acts; for " by their fruits ye shall know them," and 'the tree which has not brought forth good fruit shall be hewn down and cast into the fire.'

The Patriot party, in carrying forward their purpose to plant in America " a more free " or "popular course of government," as a refuge from the absolute power and tyranny then aimed at by king and court, had to contend against the constant opposition of the Court party, and unfortunately for the truth of history they had no public control over the evidences. The press was not free to them; they could only preserve copies of their own records by stealth; they not only did not publish the history of their great movement, but evidently would not have been permitted to do so; for all of their records upon which an authentic history could have been based were taken from them by the opponent Court party, with the manifest purpose of making it impossible for the truth regarding their popular political enterprise ever to be known.

The first "histories" of this enterprise were published under the auspices of the Court party, composed of those who were then upholding "the kingly power," and opposing the political principles which were inspiring the movement. This party was armed with royal authority over persons and papers; it possessed an absolute control over all evidences, and used this control to its own partisan purposes. It had the power "to take and to keep" all of the records of the first "body politic" of our country, and exercised it. It had the power to publish to the world an incomplete, incorrect, *ex parte* account purporting to be the history of the great political reform movement to which the crown was bitterly opposed, and made use of it; and it had the power to require an acceptation of crown evidences as reliable authority, and virtually did so.

We have been living for more than a century under the fully developed idea of the Patriot party for a popular course of government in America, which the Court party wished to destroy in chrysalis, and we know that it is good fruit. We now know that if a correct contemporary history of the acts and objects of the Patriot party, written by a capable historian in sympathy with the grand purposes of their great movement, had been available from the beginning, it would have inspired veneration for our patriotic founders, appreciation for their noble sacrifices, admiration for their political purposes, and a proper desire to perpetuate their memories. And we now also know that such a history would not have been licensed under the crown in 1624, because these were the very sentiments which the Court party wished to obliterate forever, and which the history licensed under the crown did obliterate.

Historians have continued to accept a large portion of the licensed history; have written our earliest history largely on crown evidences, without regard for the managers of the business, or for the fact that their evidences were wanting; and so entirely without regard for the political conditions obtaining under the crown that they have overlooked the royal idea that the honors for the services of the agents or representatives of a king really belonged to the king himself; and therefore "history" has conveyed even a more belittling idea than the Court party intended it to convey. The founding of this great country, instead of being regarded as the lasting monument to King James I., as the Court party contended, and as the Rev. Samuel Purchas plainly regarded it in his works, has come to be considered as a lasting monument to John Smith in his personal instead of in his official capacity. Personally he was a man of straw, of no authority, means, or influence; while officially he was a representative of James I. (the crown), from whom he derived his authority both as a councilor in Virginia and as a historian in England, and to whom (James I.), in the view of the censors of the press, the honors for his services really belonged, and as they thought were really given. And, therefore, if the "history" is true they should be so given.

The history licensed by the crown failed to create in the colony a desire to return to the form of government designed for the plantations by James I. as administered by the historian, and it failed to destroy the faith in "the popular course of government" to which the historian was opposed; but in many respects it has done about all the harm that its sponsors wished it to do. Instead of being a fair account of the beginning of the most important political reform movement of modern times, it is a mere eulogy of the "historian," a traduction of the original of the body politic of this nation, and a stigma upon the popular political principles which inspired them. It has really reversed the true view of our national origin; given the chief honors to the chief agent in perpetrating the historic wrong; censured those who deserved praise, robbed our patriotic founders of the honors due them, and deprived our origin of its inspiring features. Instead of fostering worthy sentiments regarding our patriotic founders and national foundation as a true patriotic history would have done, it has caused an entire misunderstanding of the beginning of the great reform political movement, and taken from the splendid fabric of our institutions the part which was due to the patriotism, the valor, and the genius of the first designers of the popular course of government for this nation.

I doubt if any citizen of this Republic has ever made a pilgrimage into "the free land of Kent," to the grave of Sir Edwin Sandys, who drafted the first idea of our constitution, and done homage there. I doubt if many have visited the old meeting places in London of the Virginian (American) courts, "the Seminary of Sedition" of the Court party, and the cradle of American freedom, wherein our first political charter rights were nurtured. And in America, the anniversary of the signing and of the landing in South Virginia of the first charter drafted by the primary designers of a liberal government for this nation has never been celebrated. The historic ceremony in the church at Jamestown, on June 2 (N. S.), 1610, has never been enshrined in song or story, or illustrated in picture. The inauguration of our national political idea on American soil has never been honored. "Not one stone has been set upon another," so to speak, to mark the planting of the seed of a popular course of government in this country.

The licensed history preserved the portraits — real or imaginary — of Queen Elizabeth, King James, Prince Charles; of the Kings of Paspahegh, Pamaunkees, and Powhatans; of the Princess Pocahontas; of the Duchess of Richmond and Lenox (who patronized the book and wished to marry the king whose political ideas the book supported); and of Captain John Smith (on several occasions), who represented the king in Virginia, and wrote or compiled the book. But the book does not preserve the picture of a single one of our patriotic founders, who at the expense of their own blood and treasure instituted the popular course of government in this country.

The methods of the crown for obliterating everything pertaining to this popular movement took such complete effect that there has not been preserved an authentic relic of a single member of the King's Council in Virginia (1607-1609) who protested against the king's form of government for Virginia, or of a single member of the first General Assembly ever convened in America. Not even the site of the grave of a single one of them is known. Not even a chair has been preserved from The Deliverance, which brought our original constitutional charter to our shores, or, with the exception of The Mayflower, from an hundred other ships sent out under the original body politic. Absolutely nothing has been done to show to the Old World that the people of this new Republic appreciate the services of the patriotic managers of the business — in England and in Virginia — on whom the enterprise depended for so long. Nothing has been done in acknowledgment of their divine inspiration, their self-sacrifices, their great expenditures, their determination in the face of the opposition of Spain, their firmness in the controversies with the king, council, commissioners, courts, and critics in

England; or of their dauntless courage in meeting all the dangers and difficulties — known or unforeseen — in England, in Europe, on the ocean, and in Virginia, with constant resolution, until, "by the mercies of God," they succeeded in their "projected ends." No memorial has ever been erected in this Republic — not even in the original boundary of the first Republic in America between 34° and 40° north latitude, extending from ocean to ocean, through the very centre of the present United States — to those who, at the expense of their own blood and treasure, first planted the seed of a more free government in this country, which germinated in "our sacred soil," and grew strong in our "free air" from a tender plant to the great tree which still flourishes, —

"And like a mountain cedar spreads its branches
To all the plaines about it!"

Such is the evil effect of royal politics on our patriotic history; such the fruit brought forth by the continued acceptance in the Republic of the historic wrongs done our founders in the history licensed by the crown. And there can be but little doubt that if James I. had succeeded in fastening the form of government designed by him for the colonies as securely on this country, the result would have been as disastrous to our political institutions as the acceptation of the account licensed by his censors has been to the history of the institution of the political principles on which the nation was founded. And the evil effect of royal politics on the history of our founders of 1606–1624, when planting the seed, enables us to see the importance of having history accurately written from the correct political point of view, and what would have been the historic fate of our forefathers of the Revolution of 1774–1783, when gathering the fruits, if they had failed to secure our charter rights, and if our history of the culmination of the grand movement had remained under the absolute control of the advocates of the old monarchical forms of government.

The work of the Court party has not brought forth good fruit, and "it should be hewn down and cast into the fire." The High Commission under James I. which licensed the publication of the book compiled by or in the name of Captain John Smith, pretending to be our earliest history, would have cast a true history of this popular movement "into the fire." It was really practically obliterated for generations. The loyal point of view of our earliest history was reversed in 1776, when we declared our independence from the crown of Great Britain, and it is high time for that history to be rescued from the acts of the agents of King James I. "Beware of false prophets, which come to you in sheep's clothing, but inwardly are ravening wolves."

The first English colony in the present United States — our political mother — was not founded by a king, nor by an agent of a king, nor on the monarchical principles of government advocated by a king, as the royal commissioners and licensed historians asserted: it was founded by patriotic statesmen, politicians, and planters on the liberal political principles advocated by them, a fact which James I. wished to obliterate forever. Under conditions which I have explained, the first historian — a paper tiger — deprived the Patriots of the honors due them in history, and subsequent historians have been doing the same thing ever since; but justice and patriotism, political principles and direct evidences, reason and circumstantial evidences are now all combined in requiring our national history to rest on its true political basis.

In conclusion, and to make the case clearer, let us review some of its features. It will have been seen that in order to understand our earliest history it is necessary to understand the political conditions then obtaining and the authority exercised by those directly interested in upholding the different political views on the colonial movement. Historians, while upholding the history licensed under the crown, have been disposed to undervalue the contemporary influence of the king who controlled the press. The high estimation in which James I. was held by the Court party will be found, not only in Purchas, but also in the preface of James Montagu, bishop of Winchester, to the 1616 edition of the king's works; in the funeral sermon, on "Great Britain's Solomon," preached by Lord Keeper John Williams in Westminster Abbey in 1625; and in many other publications, as well as in crown evidences still in manuscript. In comparing James I. to Solomon, it seems evident that Williams thought James I. the greater man. Like Purchas and other members of the Court party, he gave to the king the credit for having spread the religion, the commerce, and the colonies of England in Asia, Africa, and America. And he did not consider it necessary to mention the name of a single one of the king's agents in these premises, or of those who had actually done the work at their own expense.

The meanings given to such words as 'King,' 'Parliament,' 'Prerogative,' etc., by the Court party at that time will be found in "The Interpreter," a book containing "the signification of words" (a law dictionary), published by Dr. John Cowell in 1607, or early in 1608. This book asserted that the English government was an absolute monarchy, and gave alarm to the members of the Patriot party, 'who were opposed to the absolute monarchy then aimed at by the king and the Court party.' It was in the winter of 1608–1609 that this party petitioned for our charter of 1609. When Parliament next met, in February, 1610, the Commons protested against Cowell's book, and although James I. finally proclaimed against it, and had it burnt by the common hangman, this was evidently diplomacy on his part, as he really believed in the monarchical principles of the book. When he addressed the judges in the Court of Star Chamber in the summer of 1616, he told them that 'on coming into England a stranger, he had resolved with Pythagoras to keep silence seven years and acquaint himself with the laws of the kingdom; and that he had delayed another seven years waiting for the proper time; but having served this double apprenticeship, he then considered himself a fit judge in the premises,'—and he proceeded to deliver a long discourse on his ideas of government, in which he impugned the Common Law of England about as much as Cowell had done, asserting that 'his own prerogative was next in place to the deity,' etc. It was about this time — certainly as early as November, 1616 — that he began to interfere with the government which the Virginia Corporation proposed to institute in this country, and he continued to do so as long as he lived. And it came to pass that the evidences disseminated under his rule have continued to be accepted as conveying a true account of the origin of this nation. There is no absolute control over histories now as was the case while the colony was under the crown, and books disseminating the ideas of the Court party cannot be burnt, nor their authors imprisoned; but there is no longer any reason why our national foundation, our founders, their acts or motives, should be presented to our people in our histories as they were pictured by the opponents of the political principles on which our country was founded. Thanks to those principles our historians are now free to correct the false ideas of the inauguration of those principles in this country which have been derived from royal historians. Thanks to those principles our press is not now obliged to publish histories of our foundation as licensed or decreed by any party in opposition to those principles. Thanks to those principles our body politic (our people) is now free and independent; our persons and papers are no longer under the absolute control of the agents of an absolute power. And when the patriotic politicians, statesmen, and people who are now upholding those principles in this fully developed Republic understand the importance of the beginning of the movement for settling a popular course of government in America, they will erect at some proper place a suitable monument as a national memorial to those Patriots who rescued the first colony from 'His Majesty's most Princely government for the direction of the affairs of the plantation by thirteen councellors in Virginia, and as many in England, all nominated by His Majesty,' — which was the real "misgovernment" in the opinion of the Patriots, — and at the expense of their own blood and treasure, regardless of the opposition of his majesty and his agents, first deposited in the womb of the great North American wilderness the germ of the vital principle which has sustained this nation since its birth — " *Vox populi, vox Dei!*"

INDEX

INDEX

Additional information regarding most of the persons mentioned will be found in "The Genesis of the United States" and "The First Republic in America."

ABBOT, GEORGE, Archbishop of Canterbury, 83, 85, 197; Maurice, 32, 196, 222.
Abdy, Anthony, 196, 222.
Accomak, 120.
Acts of General Assembly. See General Assembly.
Act of Parliament, 36-39, 49-52, 93. See Parliament.
Adams, John, 144; Henry, 171.
Adventurers of the purse and of the person, 222-227. See Virginia Corporation and Body Politic.
Alabama, 207.
Albany (N. Y.), 169.
Albemarle Co., Va., 159, 160.
Aldersgate, 28.
America, North, 1, 6-12, 14, 15, 22, 24, 25, 28, 29, 37, 53, 55, 60, etc.; South, 55, etc.
American Antiquarian Society, 169, 170; colonization, 183; continent, 216; freedom, 254; government, 209, 220; liberty, 146, 147, 216; Magna Charta, 29; movement, 10, 14; soil, 17, 254; talisman, 16, 20, 56; wilderness, 12, 262.
Anderson's "History of the Colonial Church," 166.
Anglo-Saxon, 39.
Annapolis, 124.
Anniversary (The), 16, 254.
Aragon, 96.
Arber, Edward, and his edition of Smith's works, 176, 177.
Archbishops of Canterbury and York, 109.

Archer, Gabriel, 9, 76, 77.
Argall, Samuel, 27, 196.
Ariel, 16.
Arizona, 207.
Arkansas, 207.
Arlington, Earl of. See Bennett.
Ashton, John, and his Life of Smith, 176.
Assembly. See General Assembly.
Atlantic, 13, 241.
Auditors, 71, 222, 223.

Bacon, Sir Francis, 9, 11, 22.
Bacon's Assembly, 235, 236; Rebellion, 120, 137, 139.
Baltimore, Lord. See Cecil and George Calvert.
Baltimore's, Lord, patent, 99, 218.
Bancroft, George, historian, 173; Richard, Archbishop of Canterbury, 15.
Barber, Gabriel, 70, 97.
Bargrave, John, 41, 46, 47, 54.
"Basilikon Doron," 9.
Bateman, Robert, 196.
Bathori, Sigismund, 95.
Bedford Co., Va., 158, 160.
Bell, Robert, 196.
Bennet, or Bennett, Henry, Earl of Arlington, 119; Richard, 107, 108, 114, 139.
Berblock, William, 45, 70.
Berkeley, Sir William, 104-106, 108, 116, 118, 120.
Bermoothes, 16.
Bermuda or Bermudas, 20, 21, 37, 77,

79; Islands Company, 46, 112. See Somers Island.
Beverley, Robert, and his history of Virginia, 122, 123, 160, 202.
Biography, 240-242.
Birch's "Court and Times of James I.," 166.
Bland, Edward, and his "Discovery of New Britaine," 111, 139; Giles, 139; John, Sr., 70, 139; John, Jr., 139; Col. Richard, 138-140, his "Inquiry," etc., 138, and his library, 140, 157.
Body Politic, — the original. See Virginia Corporation.
Bond, Martin, 196.
Boston, 170.
Boundary rights, 147-150. See Charter rights.
Brewster, Edward, 20.
Briggs, Henry, 222.
British Museum, 166, 168.
Broadsides, 19, 62.
Brooke, Christopher, 32, 34.
Brown, Alexander, an explanation, 175, 178-190, 212-215.
Bryant and Gay, historians, 173.
Buck, Rev. Richard, 17, 18, 20.
Buckingham, Duke of. See Villiers.
Buckner, John, 121.
Burgesses. See House of Burgesses.
Butler, Nathaniel, 127, 196.
Byrd, Col. William the 1st, 135-137; the 2d, 135-139; the 3d, 138-140; their library, 140.

Cæsar, Sir Julius, master of the King's Rolls (Records), 196.
Calendars. See State Papers.
California, 207.
Calvert, Cecil, 2d Lord Baltimore, 98, 99, 149, 150, 163; George, Secretary of State, 1st Lord Baltimore, 196.
Cambell (or Campbell), James, 196.
Cambridge (Mass.), 166, 170.
Camden Society of England, 169.
Campbell's, Charles, History of Virginia (1860), 118.

Canning, William, 114, 128.
Canterbury, 15, 83, 85, 99, 109, 197.
Carew, George Lord, 55; his letters to Roe, 169.
Carie (Carey, Cary), Sir Philip, 196.
Carleton, Sir Dudley, 96, 167.
Carter's Mountain, 159.
Cartwright, Abraham, 196.
Cavalier, 107.
Cavendish, William, Lord (afterwards Earl of Devonshire), 32, 42, 44, 46, 114.
Chalmers, George, 156.
Chambers, George, 35, 222.
Charles, Prince, 37, 43, 50, 254; King, I., 89-103, 89, 91-94, 96, 98, 99, 101-107, 113, 133, 134, 138, 139, 148, 155, 162, 211, 213, 248; his Proclamation, 91, 92; II., 108, 114, 116-119, 121, 122, 134, 139, 235.
Charters, 242, 248; (of 1606), 6-8, 17, 21, 22, 48, 77, 78, 126, 148, 160, 161, 205, 206, 208, 209, 216, 232; (of 1609), 6-13, 16, 17, 21-24, 52-56, 78, 126, 127, 130-132, 143, 146, 148-150, 161-163, 204-216, 218, 220, 230-232; (of 1612), 21-24, 52-56, 78, 126, 127, 130-132, 143, 146, 148, 161, 162, 204, 205, 207, 209-216, 220, 222, 232; (of 1620, N. E.), 101, 210, 212; (of 1621, Va.), 35-40, 211; (of 1629, Mass.), 45, 143, 207, 211-213; (of 1631, Va.), 97, 98; (of 1640, Va.), 103, 104, 107.
Charter rights, liberal, political, and property, 13, 17, 204-216, 242; efforts to protect by Act of Parliament, 35-41, 49, 52; contest over, between the Court and Patriot parties, 27, 32, 35, 36, 38, 40, 42-56, 59, 67, 85, 89-108, 118-121, 140-150, 153, 154, 193, 195, 226, 227, 234, 242-244; secured by our Revolution, 13, 55, 142-147, 149, 153, 154, 184, 257. See Petitions.
Chichester, Arthur Lord, 55, 196.
Church of England, 182, 244, 247.
Cities of England, 35.
Civil War of England, 104-108.
Claiborne, William, 100, 107, 114.

INDEX

Clarendon, Earl of. See Edward Hide.
Clark, George Rogers, 149.
Climate of Virginia, 218.
Collingwood, Edward, 65.
Colonial Commission under Charles I. (Liberal), 96-99; Laud's, 99.
Commissions. See King's Commissions.
Commons, House of, 9, 36-40, 51, 60, 94, 103-105, 117, 138, 140, 202, 248, 260. See Parliament.
Commons Journal, 38, 39, 60.
Commonwealth, 106-108, 111, 139, 165, 201.
"Company of English merchants," 221.
Congress, 156.
Constitution, the Corporations, 16, 127. See, under Virginia.
Constitution, the king's, 77, 126.
Contest (continued) between the Court and Patriot parties over charter rights, 42-49.
Controversy, the, between the Court and Patriot parties becomes an open contest over the reform movement, 30-35.
Conway, Sir Edward, Secy. of State, 196.
Cooke, John Esten, and his "Virginia," 176.
Copeland, Rev. Patrick, 45.
Coppinford, 134.
Corporation. See under Massachusetts, New England, Pilgrims, and Virginia.
Corporations, 97, 99.
Council. See Privy Council, and under Virginia.
Court party. See under Parties, National.
Courts. See High Commission; King's Bench; Star Chamber; Virginia.
Coventry, Thomas, Lord, Attorney-General, 36, 54, 99, 196, 211, 226.
Cowell, Rev. Dr. John, 259, 260.
Cranfield, Lionel, Earl of Middlesex, 50, 66, 89, 90, 195.
Cranmer, William, 32, 35, 222.

Cromwell, Oliver, 105, 107; Richard, 107.
Crown of England (Great Britain), 45, 48, 59, 106, etc., 227, 248.
Crown, the, annuls the Virginia charters, 52-56; confiscates the evidences, 59-69; licenses the history, 73-86. See under Evidences, James I., Charles I., Charles II., and George III.
Culpeper, Thomas, Lord, 119, 121.

Dale, Sir Thomas, 114, 238.
Danvers, Henry, Earl of Danby, 97; Sir John, 32-34, 70, 71, 91, 97, 102, 103, 111-114, 133, 139, 222; his copies of the Va. Court Records (1619-1624), 71, 72, 91, 133-140, 157.
Davison, Christopher, 66.
Deane, Charles, 166, 169-171, 174, 175.
Declarations, 62; of 1609, 19; of 1610, 166; of 1620, 223-225; of 1623, 44; of 1624, 104; of 1642, 104, 105; of Independence, 143, 144.
Delaware (State), 207.
De la Warr, Lord. See West.
Deliverance, the, 16, 255.
Democracie of England, 107.
Dennis, Robert, 107.
D'Evereux, Robert, 2d Earl of Essex, 14, 15.
Devonshire, Earl of. See Cavendish,
Devonshire [William Cavendish, 5th], Duke of, 147.
Dichfield, Edward, 197.
Digges, Sir Dudley, 97; Edward, 108.
Discovery, the, 241.
"Dispatch," The Richmond, Va., 175.
District of Columbia, 207.
Doncaster, Lord. See James Hay.
Donne, George, 101; Rev. Dr. John, 101.
Dorchester, Viscount. See D. Carleton.
Dorset, Earl of. See E. Sackville.
Doyle, J. A., and his " English Colonies in America," 175.
Dunmore's War, 149.

Dutch man-of-war, 167.
Dyke, John, 166.

East Greenwich, 27.
Edmonds, Sir Thomas, treasurer of the king's household, 196.
Edwards, Richard, 196.
Efforts to protect charter rights by Act of Parliament, 35-41, 49-52; to annul our charter rights, 52-56; to preserve evidences, 69-73; to obliterate the true history of our national origin, 59-69, 73-86, 129, 130, 238, 239, 250-253.
Eggleston, Edward, and his "Pocahontas," 173.
Election, freedom of, 32, 33, 42, 43, 45-48.
Elizabeth, queen of England, 14, 109, 198, 254.
Emigrants. See Planters.
England, 1, 6-10, 14-16, 19, 24, 30, 34, 40-43, 52-54, etc.; common law of, 260; crown of. See Crown.
English, the, 10, 11, etc.; colony, 15, 21, 30, 31, 54, etc.; American plantations, 19; constitution, 10, 23, 143, etc.; government, 259; history, 26; rights, advocates of. See Patriot Party.
English politics in early Virginia history, *passim*.
Enterprise under the government of James I., 6, 7. See Government.
Episcopalians, 244.
Essex, Earl of. See D'Evereux.
Essington, William, 222.
Europe, 215.
Evidences, controlled by the crown, 3-5, 59-86, 108-116, 225, 229, 238, 242-257; of the Virginia Corporation, 61-64, 73, 90, 91, 122, 123, 126-128, 133-140, 155, 157, 162, 194-204, 224. See Historic Wrong.

Fairfax, Lord, 163.
Fanshaw, Thomas, 195.
Farrar (see Ferrar), Thomas, 159.
Ferrar, Edward, Sr., 165; Edward, Jr., 165; John, Sr., 28, 30, 36, 38, 45- 47, 53, 54, 97, 102, 111, 112, 114, 133, 134, 165, 194, 222; his memoir of his brother Nicholas, 114, 165; John, Jr., 165; Mrs. Mary, 92; Nicholas, Jr., 28, 35, 45-47, 50, 51, 67, 71, 89-92, 97, 109-110, 112, 114, 133, 165, 194; his copies of the Records of the Virginia Corporation (1609-1624?), 71, 72, 90, 91, 98, 133; William of Virginia, 100.
Ferrars, the, 92, 99; their house, 37; their influence, 106.
First republic in America (territory of), 12, 213, 256.
"First Republic in America" (book), 8, 13, 25, 29, 34, 35, 39, 42, 67, 76, 84, 85, 114, 127, 133, 170, 179, 184, 185, 187, 194, 197, 210-212, 215.
First: fleet of 1606, 7, 241; charter for our original body politic, 13-16; inauguration of the reform movement, 13-21, 254; fleet of the corporation (1609), 16, 19, 241; constitution, 16; anniversary, 16; steps in planting liberty in America, 17; sermon, 18; governor, 19; joint stock, 25; inauguration of the reform government, 26-29, 254; effort to protect our charter rights by Act of Parliament, 35-41; charters, published in 1747, 132; House of Burgesses, 146, 255, account of, published in 1857, 167; English colony in America, 193, 221, 227, 228, 258; Plymouth patent, 210; Englishmen to teach Indians the use of arms, 224, 225; histories, 250; political charter rights, 254; planted the seed, etc., 256; mission to England for charter rights, 52; etc.
Fiske, John, 173.
Force, Peter, his reprints, 166.
Fortune, the, 210.
Foundation, our national. See under English Politics.
Founders, our. See the Patriot party.
France, 125, 149, 150, 158, 204, 244.
Free air of America, 76, 246, 256.
"Freedom of election," 32, 33, 42,

INDEX

43, 45-48; American, 254; "freely elected," 231, 235.
Freeman, Raphe, 196.
Free-trader, 219.
French and Indian War, 149.
Fruit produced by the acts of the Patriot party, 250, 251; by the acts of the Court party, 252-257.
Fuller, Rev. Thomas, and his "Worthies," 117, 174.

Gainsborough. See Noel.
Galthorpe, Stephen, 76.
Gardiner's "History of England," 8, 109.
Gates, Sir Thomas, 15-21, 77, 79, 114, 160, 161, 238.
Gay, historian, 173.
General Assembly in Virginia, 29, 34, 52, 53, 66, 93, 94, 101, 102, 104-108, 126, 146, 157, 167, 232, 233, 235, 255.
"Genesis of the United States" (The), 18, 19, 25, 96, 170, 180-184, 215, 223.
George III., 140-147, 155.
Georgia, 207.
Gibbs, Thomas, 32, 97, 196.
Goad, Rev. Thomas, 83.
Goethe, 178.
Gofton, Sir F., 196.
Gondomar, Spanish ambassador, 30, 31, 35, 37, 42, 43, 46, 55, 219.
Gorges, Sir F., 196, 210.
Gosnold, Capt. B., 76.
Government of the plantation under James I. (1607-1610), 6, 7, 10, 17, 19, 20, 23, 48, 55, 75-78, 84, 193, 206, 228-230, 232, 236, 237, 241, 248, 255, 256; proposed by the king in 1624, 55, 256.
Government of Ireland, 55, 97; of the kings of Spain in the West Indies, 55, 97.
Government, the reform, of the colony under the corporation, the popular course, 5, 17, 21, 25-29, 34, 35, 40, 41, 43, 48, 55, 221, 229-233, 236, 237, 248, 254-258; the American idea, 17, 208, 209, 215, 216, 220.
Government, the forms of, at issue, 228-236.

Gowrie Conspiracy, 60, 61, 197.
Grandison. See Oliver St. John.
Graves, Thomas, 17.
Great Britain, 12, 106, 122, 149, 244, 257.
"Great Britain's Solomon," 259.
Great Charter. See Magna Charta.
Great Mogul, 169.
Green Bag (magazine), 29.
Greenwich, East, 27.
Grigsby's Virginia Convention of 1776, 138.
Grindon, Edward, 224.
Gunpowder Plot, 60, 61.

Hackwell or Hakewell, William, 196, 220.
Hakluyt Society, England, 166.
Hale, Rev. E. E., 169.
Hamilton, James, Marquess of, 37, 47.
Hamor, Ralph, 18; his "Discourse," 169.
Hampshire, England, 91, 134.
Hampton Court Conference, 8.
Handford (or Handsford), Sir Humphrey, 196, 222.
Harvey, Sir John, 52, 66, 94-97, 100-102, 104, 115, 127.
Harwood, Sir Edward, 45; Thomas, 100.
Hawes, Michael, 196.
Hay, James, Lord Doncaster, 32, 36.
Hayman, Sir Peter, 38.
Heath, Sir Robert, the king's Solicitor-General, 35, 149, 196.
Hening, Wm. Waller, and his Virginia Statutes, 104, 118, 154, 155.
Henry, Hon. W. W., 172-175, 187.
Herbert, Edward, 32, 34, 36, 70; George, the poet, 92, 109, 112; Philip, Earl of Pembroke, 105; William, Earl of Pembroke, 15, 32, 37, 47.
Hertford. See Seymour.
Hickes, Sir Baptist, 196.
Hickman, Richard, 138, 156, 157.
Hide or Hyde, Lawrence, 32; Edward, Earl of Clarendon, 137.
High Commission, 65, 83-85, 109, 110, 197, 199, 202, 257.

270 INDEX

Historians licensed by the crown. See Rev. S. Purchas and Captain J. Smith.

Historic wrong done our patriotic founders by James I., his commissioned officers, and licensed historians: By the suppression of evidences favorable to the popular movement of 1609-1624, and unfavorable to the king's administration of 1606-1609, and the preservation and dissemination of evidences favorable to the administration of James I. (1606-1609) and unfavorable to the reform movement of the Patriots, 5, 59-69, 73-86, 90, 91, 95-97, 108, 109, 113, 115-117, 119, 121-132, 141, 142, 153, 194-205, 217; how the wrong was perpetuated under the crown, 89-150, and under the Republic, 153, 154, 164, 165, 170-178, 185-189, 212, 213. The efforts to correct the wrong under the crown, 69-73, 90, 91, 95, 98, 108, 111-115, 126-128, 132-140, 142, 154, 156, 157; and under the Republic, 153-158, 165-169, 178-190, 212-215, 257-262. A summary of the political features of the historic wrong, 190-256.

"Historical Magazine," The, 171.

History, control over by the crown, 108-116; importance of the political point of view in, 249-262; licensed by the crown, 73-86, 95, 228, 237, 250. See Smith's "Generall Historie."

"History of our Earliest History," 187.

Hobart, Sir Henry, 11, 22.

Holborn, 65, 134.

Holland, 215.

Holles, John, Lord Houghton, 43.

Hopkins, Stephen, 18.

Hopton, Ralph, 117.

Horsmanden, Mary, 137; Warham, 138.

Horwood. See Harwood.

Hothersall, Thomas, 161.

Houghton, Lord. See Holles.

House of Burgesses in Virginia, 29, 93, 94, 100, 108, 117-119, 121, 138, 140, 146, 167, 231, 235, 236. See General Assembly.

House of Commons. See Commons.

House of Lords. See Lords.

Howard, Francis, Lord, 121.

Howes, Edmond, his publications, 82.

Huguenots, 244.

Huntingdonshire, 92.

Illinois, 207.

Inaugurating the reform movement, 13-21; the reform government, 26-29.

Incorporations. See Corporations.

Independent. See Patriot party.

Indian Territory, 207.

Indiana, 207.

Indians, 12, 25, 27, 43, 80 120, 149, 218, 224, 225, 240.

Infanta of Spain, 37.

Influence of contemporary politics on history as enacted, 1-56; as published, 59-86; of subsequent politics in upholding the historic wrong, under the crown, 89-147, and under the Republic, 153-180.

"Interpreter" (The), 259, 260.

Introductory, 3-5.

Ireland, 45, 50, 53, 55, 97, 195, 244.

James I., 1, 5-13, 15, 17, 22-24, 26, 28, 29, 31-33, 35-40, 42-46, 48-51, 53, 55-57, 59, 60, 65-68, 72-80, 83-86, 89, 90, 92-94, 97, 99, 104, 109, 113, 116, 117, 119, 120, 122, 123, 126-129, 131, 132, 136, 145-149, 153, 155, 160-163, 165-168, 170, 176, 177, 182, 183, 185, 187-189, 193-195, 197-200, 202-204, 206, 210, 212-214, 216, 217, 219, 221, 223, 229-233, 236, 237, 241, 245, 248, 249, 252-254, 256-262; his "Basilikon Doron," 9; "True Law of Free Monarchies," 9; "Premonition to all most mighty Monarchs," 9; "Remonstrance for the Rights of Kings," 26; his form of government for the Colonies and Companies. See under Government;

King's Commissions, Councils, etc.
James II., 122.
James River, 21, 159.
Jamestown, 16-21, 29, 52, 94, 166, 208, 254.
Jefferson, John, 52; Thomas, 110, 137, 139-141, 144, 146, 150, 227; a laborer in the field of original research, 153-158; his library, 140; his "Notes on Virginia," 158-164.
Jermyn, Philip, 34, 196.
Johnson, Edward, 196; Robert, 13, 30, 32, 44, 114, 127, 196.
Joint, or common stock, 25-27, 218, 219, 222.
Jones, Sir William, 45, 67, 195.

Kansas, 207.
Keightley, Thomas, 32, 222.
Keith, Sir William, his History of Virginia, 123, 160, 202.
Kendall, George, 76.
Kent, 38, 39, 50.
Kentucky, 207.
Killigrew, Sir Robert, 70, 91, 97, 98, 133, 196.
King, of the Pamaunkees, 254; of Paspahegh, 254; of the Powhatans, 254; of England. See James I.
King's Bench, Court of, 53, 83, 98, 124, 195, 212.
King's Commissioners in England, 45-49, 53, 67, 82, 195; in Virginia, 52, 65-67, 94, 104, 115, 116, 127, 195.
King's Council in Virginia (1607-1610), 7, 17, 75-78, 193, 206, 229, 230, 237, 241, 255.
Kirkham, Robert, 32.

Lands granted, 12, 13, 22.
Lane, Ralph, 245.
Laud, William, Archbishop of Canterbury, 99, 109; his chaplain, 109.
Law (Common), of England, 260.
Leate, or Leake, Nicholas, 196.
Lee [R. H.], 144.
Lefroy, General Sir J. H., 173.
Leiger Court Books, 71.
Lewis, Andrew, 149.
Ley, Sir James, 53, 67, 195.

Liberal ideas of government. See Reform Government.
Liberal political charter rights. See Charter rights.
Liberal party. See Patriot party.
"Liberties," 39; Liberty, 13, 17, 115, 146, 147, 216, 246, 248; "Liberty of the Subject," 220.
Library of Congress, 140, 157, 158.
Lilburne, John, 110; Robert, 110; William, 110.
Little Gidding, 92, 99, 133.
Lisle, Lord. See Sidney.
Lodge, Hon. H. C., 173.
London (the capital), 27-29, 92, 96, 110, 122, 127, 134, 147, 162, 166-168, 173, 233, 254. See Virginia Corporation, commonly called The Virginia Company of London, the Virginia Courts in London, etc.
Lords, House of, 38, 40, 140, 146. See Parliament.
Lotteries, 223.
Ludwell, Thomas, 119.
Lymington, 50.

"Magazine of American History" (N. Y.), 133.
Magna Charta, 29, 162.
Mallory, Sir James, 38.
Managers of the business, 13, 26, 46, 62, 84, 89, 90, 217, 236-244, 246, 249-251, 255, 256; their Discourse, 89-91. See Virginia Corporation and Virginia Courts.
Managers of the government for the crown, 217, 237.
Manchester. See Montagu.
Mansfield, Sir Robert, 15.
Marbois, Mons. De, 158.
Marlier, or Martian, Nicholas, 100.
Martin, Capt. John, 17, 26, 49, 77.
Maryland, 98, 99, 124, 141, 149, 163, 207, 218.
Massachusetts, 166, 170, 174, 211-213; charter, 45, 96, 207, 211-213, 233; corporation, 212-214; Historical Society, 165. See Virginia (North).
Massacre by the Indians, 43.

INDEX

Matthews, Samuel, 52, 100, 101, 103, 114.
Maurice of Nassau, 19, 20.
May, Sir H., 196.
Mayflower, the, 205; compact, 209.
McLeod, Captain, 158.
Meeting places of the Virginia courts, 254. See House of the Ferrars, Sir E. Sandys, Sir Thos. Smith, and the Earl of Southampton. See London.
Menefie, George, 100.
Mexico, 150.
Middlesex. See Cranfield.
Mildmay, Sir Henry, 44, 196; John, 196.
Milton, John, 111, 117; his "Areopagitica," 111.
Mississippi River, 149, 150; State, 207.
Missouri, 207.
Mogul, the Great, 169.
Mole, George, 196.
"Monarchie," 47, 49; Old World, 208.
"Monarchies, True Law of Free," 9.
"Monarchs, Premonition to all most mighty," 9.
Monarchy, absolute, 259. See under Government.
Monopolies, 219, 220; monopolist, 219.
Montagu, Sir Charles, 196; Edward, Earl of Manchester, 105; Henry Viscount Mandeville, etc., 196; James, bishop, 259.
Monticello, 139, 158, 160, 161.
Moore, Sir George, 39.
Morer, Richard, 197.
Morryson, Francis, 119.
Movement, the motive of the reform, 245-249; the correct political and historical point of view of, 180-189, 249-262. See Reform movement.
Mulberryes, 218.
Mulberry Island, 20.

Neill, Rev. E. D., his "Virginia Company," 172.

Netherlands, 15, 19, 72, 91, 125, 163, 204.
Nevada, 207.
New England, 82, 95, 101, 183, 210, 212, 213. See Charter, 1620; Virginia (North).
New Jersey, 207.
"New Life of Virginia," 25, 165.
New Mexico, 207.
New World, 5, 17, 24, 53, 208, 216, 248.
New York, 169; documents, 167; Historical Society, 167; magazine, 171.
Newport, Captain C., 18, 21, 76; his ".Discoveries," 169.
Neyle, Richard, Archbishop of York, 99.
Noel, Edward, Earl of Gainsborough, 135; Lady Elizabeth, 134; Wriothesley, Earl of Gainsborough, 135.
Nonconformists, 244.
"North American Review," 171.
North Carolina, 149, 207.
Northern Neck of Va., 117, 119, 163.
North Virginia. See Virginia (40° to 45° n. l.), North.
Northumberland [Hugh Smithson Percy], Duke of, 147.
"Notes and Queries," London, 96.
Notes on the way, 1660 to 1746, 116-124.
Nottingham, 105.
"Nova Britannia," 14, 166.

Obtaining the first charter for the original body politic, 6-13; the second charter, 21-26.
Ogle, Sir John, 44, 45.
Ohio, 207.
Oklahoma, 207.
Old World, 215, 216, 244, 255; monarchies, 208.
Orange, Prince of, 167.
Origin of this nation. See Principles of liberty; Vis vitæ, etc.
Original of the body politic of this nation. See Virginia Corporation and Body Politic.
Oxford Tract, 79-82, 84, 85.

INDEX 273

Pacific Ocean, 23. See South Sea.
Packard, Rev. Peter, his Life of N. Ferrar, 165, 194.
Paget, William, Lord, 43, 196.
Palfrey, historian, 175.
Pallavacine, Edward, 196.
Palmer, William, 196.
Pamaunkees, King of, 254.
Paris, France, 158.
Parks, William, 124.
Parliament, 141, 144, 259, 260; First, James I., 8, 9, 35, 220; Second, James I., 35; Third, James I., 35-41; Fourth, James I., 49-52, 89, 134; First, Charles I., 93, 94; Second, Charles I., 93; Third, Charles I., 94, 109 ; Fourth, Charles I., 103; Fifth, Charles I., or Long, 103-105, 107, 108, 110, 118, 137, 202; of Charles II., 117, 118. See Commons and Lords.
Parliament in Virginia, 9, 76.
Parliamentary business, 38, 39.
Parties in the Virginia Corporation, 34, 44, 45, 51, 73. See Sir Edwin Sandys and Sir Thomas Smith.
Parties, National political: Court party which controlled the evidences and laid the foundation upon which the history has been written, 1, 5, 9, 10, 22, 24, 26, 30, 34, 37, 39, 43-46, 53, 57, 60, 66, 67, 69, 73-75, 78-82, 84-87, 95-97, 100, 101, 104-106, 108, 110, 113, 115, 117, 122, 128-132, 136, 145-147, 153, 154, 163, 165, 174, 177, 178, 181-184, 188, 189, 191, 193-195, 197, 200, 201, 204, 210, 212, 217, 219, 221, 227, 228, 234, 237, 238, 240, 242, 243, 245, 247-261; Patriot party, which managed the business and laid the foundation upon which this great nation has been erected, 1, 5, 8, 10, 24, 25, 30, 33-35, 37-40, 42-46, 48-53, 60, 69, 72, 75, 76, 79, 81, 84-87, 90-98, 103, 108, 110, 111, 113-115, 120, 122, 128-132, 136, 139, 145, 146, 153, 165, 174, 182, 184, 188-191, 194, 195, 197, 200-204, 210, 211, 226, 227, 234, 236, 242-245, 248-251, 253, 255, 258-262; evidences for, confiscated, 59-69; preserved, 69-73.
Parties in Virginia, 52, 100, 102, 105, 120, 141, 143, 144, 146, 153, 160, 163, 243, 244.
Paspahegh, King of, 254.
Past politics, influence of, 164-169. See under Political and Politics.
Patience, the, 16.
Patriot party. See under Parties, National.
Peirce. See Pierce.
Pembroke, Earl of. See Herbert.
Pennant's account of London, 135.
Pennsylvania, 149, 207.
Percy, George, 17, 78, 241.
Perry, William, 100.
Petitions for charter rights, 36, 51; (1624), 52, 92; (1625), 92, 93; (1626), 93; (1630-1632), 97, 98, 148, 149; (1633), 98, 99; (1640), 103, 104, 107, 108; (1674), 119-121; (1764), 140; (1624-1774), 234; against, 104, 105.
"Petition of Rights," 94.
Philadelphia, 143, 156, 157
Pierce, William, 18, 100.
Pierce's patent, 209.
Piersey, Abraham, 52.
Pilgrims, 15, 18, 209-212. See Virginia (North).
Planters, 7, 9, 12, 13, 17, 20, etc., 53, 225-227, 240, 241, 244, 246, 247, 258. See under Virginia Corporation and Body Politic.
Plymouth, England, 15, 16, 101.
Plymouth Patent, N. E., 210.
Pocahontas incident, 170-177, 249, 254.
Point Comfort, 19.
Political charter rights. See Charter rights; features of the historic case, 191-262; importance of the reform movement, 5-7, 10-13, 17, 22, etc.; objects, 25, 27, 28, 31, 35, 47, etc.; point of view, 240, 249-262; policies, 8-15, 33, etc.; character of the historic wrong. See Historic Wrong; influences, see Influence.
Politics in early Virginia history as represented in the acts and evi-

dences of the Court and Patriot
  parties. See Charters; Charter
  Rights; Evidences; Historic
  Wrong; Parties, National; Past
  Politics; Present Politics, etc.
Poole (see Powell), Robert, 224.
Poplar Forest, 158-160.
Popular charters. See Charters of
  1609, 1612.
Popular course of government. See
  under Government.
Popular parties. See Patriot party.
Portland [Cavendish-Bentinck],
  Duke of, 147.
Pory, John, 52, 66, 167, 196.
Pott, Dr. John, 100.
"Potter's American Monthly," 172.
Pountis, John, 52, 92, 127.
Powell, Nathaniel, 17.
Powhatans, King of, 241, 249, 254.
"Premonition to all most mighty
  Monarchs," 9.
Prerogatives of the king, 259.
Presbyterians, 244.
Present politics, influence of, 170-
  178, 212-215. See under Political,
  and Politics.
Presidents and Council in Virginia,
  230. See King's Council in Virginia.
Press, the, controlled by the crown,
  3-5, 59-61, 70, 73, 81-86, 95, 109-111,
  115, 116, 121, 122, 125, 142, 153; under
  the Commonwealth, 111-114;
  in Virginia, 115, 116, 121, 122, 124,
  125, 141, 142, 153.
Principles of liberty (immortal), 10-
  13, 17, 19, 23, 24, 31, 53, 56, etc., 201,
  228, 229, 233-237, 242-244, 257, 261,
  262. See Government (the reform); Vis vitæ, etc.
Printers. See Press.
Privy Chamber, 102.
Privy Council of the King, 36, 41, 44,
  45, 47, 50-52, 60, 61, 63, 65, 83, 90, 93,
  100, 112, 142, 168, 182, 195.
Proclamation of May, 1625, 91, 92.
Protectionist, 219.
Protestation of the Commons, 39.
Providence, 20, 56, 72, 108, 167, 202,
  234, 246-249.

Public record office, 167, 168.
Purchas, Rev. Samuel, and his publications, 81, 82, 85, 95, 125, 197,
  198, 205, 252, 259.
Puritans, 15. See Massachusetts.
Pym, John, 105.
Pythagoras, 260.

Quo Warranto, 53-55, 67, 98, 99, 120,
  226.

Radcliffe, John, 77, 241, 242.
Raleigh, Sir W., 245.
Randolph, Sir John, 136, 138, 156, 157,
  229; John of Roanoke, 157; Peyton, 156; library, 157.
Randolph's copies of the Virginia
  Court Records, 157.
Rayner, Marmaduke, 167.
Records, 71, 72, 90, 91, 98, 108-116,
  133-140, 238.
Reform charters, 204-216. See under Charters.
Reform government. See under
  Government.
Reform movement, 5-7, 10-22, 30-35,
  73, 193-204, 226, 237; motive of the,
  245-249.
Remonstrance of the most gracious
  King James I., 26; of the Commons, 9; of his Majesty's well
  wishing, 42.
Republic, the, 154, 156, 164, 165, 178,
  180, 184, 185, 187, 197, 202, 228, 242,
  253, 255, 256.
Revolution, 13, 142-147, 149, 153, 156,
  165, 202, 227, 236.
Revolutionary disputes, 141, 143;
  history, 159; leaders, 141, 143, 146.
Rich, Sir Nathaniel, 44, 46, 47, 196;
  Robert, Earl of Warwick, 44, 47,
  his house, 47.
Richard, the, 8.
Richmond, Va., 157, 166; "Dispatch," 175.
Rider, Edward, 145.
Rights, boundary, charter, historical, political, of the Patriots who
  founded this country, *passim*.
Rind, William, 141.
Robertson, W., 171.

INDEX

Rockfish River, 159.
Roe, Sir Thomas, 32, 34; Letters to, 169.
Rogers, Jane, 110.
Rolfe, Mrs. John, 18; John, 18, 174; his "Relation," 166.
Roundhead, 107, 244.
Royal Commissions, 82. See King's Commissions.
Royal MSS., 166.
Royalist party. See Court party.
Russell, Lady Rachel, Lord William, 135.
"Rymer's Fœdera," 123.

Sackville, Sir Edward, 44, 97, 98.
Saint Andrew's Church, 65.
St. John, Oliver, Viscount Grandison, 55.
Sandwich, 36.
Sandys, Sir Edwin, 8, 9, 11, 22, 27, 28, 30-34, 36-40, 44-47, 49-51, 60, 79, 82, 89, 92, 102, 113, 114, 120, 128, 129, 133, 145, 183, 200, 209, 211, 219, 222, 238, 253; his house, 28; his party, 82, 222; George, 97, 102, 103, 105, 133; Sir Samuel, 36.
Sandys-Ferrar influence, 106.
Sandys - Southampton administration (1619-1624), 62.
Scotch army, 107, 134.
Scotland, 244.
Scott, Anthony, 21; General W., 150.
Scottsville, Va., 159.
"Seating Place," 6.
Second effort to protect our charter rights by Act of Parliament, 49-52.
Seelye, Lillie Eggleston, 173.
Segar, Sir William, the King's king of arms, 95, 96.
Selden, John, 28, 34, 36, 38, 94, 109, 138.
"Seminary of Sedition," 40, 72, 127, 231, 254.
"Seminary for a seditious Parliament," 31, 143. See Virginia courts in London.
Sermons, 18, 21.
Seymour, Edward, Earl of Hertford, 80, 83, 225.
Shadwell Street, London, 110.

Shakespeare, William, and his "Tempest," 16.
Sheffield, Edmond, Lord, 32.
Sidney, Sir Philip, 15; Robert, Lord Lisle, 15.
Sigismund Bathor, 95.
Smith, Catherine, 138; John of Nibley, 45, 238; Robert of London, 35; Robert of Virginia, 119; Sir Thomas, Treasurer of the Virginia Corporation (1609-1619), 14, 15, 27, 30, 32, 41, 44, 47, 51, 81, 82, 90, 114, 128-130, 138, 196, 219, 224, 237, 238; his house in London, 81; his party, 82, 90, 128, 183, 222.
Smith, John, a historian licensed under the crown, and a representative of James I. in Virginia, 5, 49, 53, 55, 65, 74-86, 95, 117, 125, 129, 164, 165, 170-178, 181, 187, 197, 223-225, 228, 229, 237-239, 241, 249, 252, 254; his "Generall Historie," 5, 53, 65, 74-76, 83-86, 95, 122-125, 129-132, 160, 164, 171-179, 181, 187, 199-203, 205, 217, 225, 237, 245, 250-257; his Oxford Tract, 79-82, 84, 85; his "True Relation," 171; his published works, 82, 95, 164, 176, 179, 225; his biographies, 164.
"Snowden," 159.
Somers Islands Company, 65. See Bermuda.
Somers, Sir George, 16, 18.
Southampton. See Wriothesley.
Southampton House, 32, 134, 135.
South Carolina, 149, 207.
Southern Literary Messenger, 160.
South Sea, 7, 246. See Pacific Ocean.
South Virginia. See Virginia (35° to 40° n. l.)
"Soveraigne Rule," 241.
Spain, 8, 12, 13, 30, 37, 42, 43, 49, 50, 97, 125, 145, 150, 204, 239, 247, 255.
Spaniards, 8, 25, 27, 80, 240, 246.
Spanish king, 30, 97, 145; match, 37, 49; ministers, 30; party, 8, 37; plan of government for Colonies, 55, 97, 145; wrongs, 8; West Indies, 10, 30, 37.
Stagg or Stegge, Thomas, 107, 137.
Stamford, 134.

Star Chamber, 64, 65, 84, 101, 109, 110, 197, 202, 260.
State Papers, Calendars of, 168.
Stationer's Hall, 83.
Stevens, Henry, 173.
Stiles, Thomas, 196.
Stith, Rev. William, 72, 125-133, 135, 156, 157, 160, 229, 230; his "History of Virginia," 15, 124-132, 135-137, 142, 160, 229, 230, 239.
Stock. See Joint stock.
Stow, John, 82.
Strachey, William, 17, 18, 21; his "Historie of Travaile," etc., 166.
Strafford. See Wentworth.
Strype, 221.
Stuart, Ludovic, 83; Duchess of Richmond and Lenox, 83, 254.
Stuart kings. See James I. and II.; Charles I. and II.
Styles. See Stiles.
Suckling, Sir John, Comptroller of the king's household, 196.
Suffrage in Virginia, 234-236. See Election.
Sustaining influence. See Vis vitæ.
Sutcliff, Rev. Dr. M., 196.

Tarleton's command, 158, 159.
Taylor, Col. H. P., 139; Gen. Z., 150.
Taxes, 28, 47, 108, 120, 140, 232, 233, 235.
Tempest, the, 16, 241.
Tennessee, 207.
Texas, 150, 207.
Text, 18.
Titchfield, library, 91, 133-135.
"Tobacco plantation," 31.
Tomlyns, Richard, 70,
Tories, 227, 243. See Court party.
"True Law of Free Monarchies," 9.
Trust Companies, 219, 220.
Tucker, Daniel, 17.
Tufton, Sir Nicholas, 32.
Tyler, President John, 150; Prof. Moses Coit, and his "History of American Literature," 172, 173, 175.

United Provinces. See Netherlands.

United States, 150, 166, 188, 193, 215, 256, 258.
University College, London, 173.
Utah, 207.
Utie, John, 100, 101.

Velasco, Don Alonso de, 30.
Villiers, George, Duke of Buckingham, 50.
Virginia (34° to 45° n. l.), 6.
Virginia, North (40° to 45° or 48° n. l.), 8, 9, 11, 150, 206, 207, 209-212, 214, 215, 222, 247, 248. See Massachusetts; New England; Pilgrims.
Virginia, South (34° to 40° n. l.), 7-12, 15-17, 19, 21, 26-29, 37, 40, 41, 43, 47-49, 51, 54, 62, 64, 66, 69, 70, 76, 78, 79, 89, 91, 92, 99, 101, 108, 140, 150, 183, 206, 207, 210-212, 214, 215, 220, 222, 229, 235, 247, 248, 254, 255.
Virginia Company (1606-1609), 6, 22, 73, 76-78, 205, 206, 208, 209, 216-218, 227, 236, 237.
Virginia Corporation and body politic (1609-1624), 22-24, 30-34, 37-39, 44, 45, 48-54, 56, 61, 64, 65, 67, 72, 82, 84, 91, 92, 95, 97, 106, 112, 118, 123-132, 134, 136, 145-147, 155, 157, 161-163, 174, 175, 182, 193-195, 197, 202, 206, 207, 210, 212, 213, 216-228, 230, 231, 233, 234, 237, 238, 241, 247, 260. See under Evidences.
Virginia courts in London, 27, 29-36, 40-43, 46, 48, 50, 53, 62, 64, 65, 66, 70, 71, 97, 127, 133-140, 142, 143, 162, 209, 217, 219, 222, 224, 231-233, 238, 254. See "Seminary of Sedition."
Virginia business, 31, 36-38, 40, 89.
"Virginia and Maryland," 111.
"Virginia Company papers, 1621-1625," 157.
"Virginia Papers, 1606-1683," 158.
Virginia, the State of, 207; convention of 1776, 138; Constitution of 1776, 149; "Magazine of History and Biography," 26, 29, 187; His-

INDEX

torical Society, 157, 171, 173; "Reporter," 171.
Virginians, 43, 70, 93, 98. See Planters.
Vis vitæ (principles of liberty, liberal ideas of government, etc.), 10-13, 17, 19, 23, 24, 31, 53, 56, 169, 228, 229, 233-237, 242-250, 257, 258, 261, 262.
"Vox populi vox Dei," 262.

Warner, Charles Dudley, his "Study of Smith's Life," etc., 173.
Warwick, Earl of. See Rich.
Washington, George, 100, 149.
Wenman, Sir F., 20.
Wentworth, Thomas, Earl of Strafford, 104.
West, Francis, 77, 94, 114; John, 100, 101, 114; Thomas, Lord De la Warr, 15, 19-21, 29, 78, 79, 114, 238, his letter, 166, his "Relation," 168.
West Indies, 10, 97. See Spanish West Indies.
Westminster Abbey, 259.
Weston, Sir R., Chancellor of the King's Exchequer, 196.
West Virginia, 207.
White, Rev. Francis, 196; John, 28, 45, 70, 211.
William the Silent, 19, 20.
William and Mary, 122.
Williamsburg, Va., 124.

Williams, Lordkeeper John, 259.
Wilmore, George, 196.
Wingfield, Capt. E. M., 76; his "Discourse of Virginia," 166, 169, 170.
Winston, Dr. Thomas, 222.
Wiseman, Richard, 222.
Withers, Anthony, 70.
Wodenoth, Arthur, and his "Short Collections," 33, 38, 44, 54, 92, 111-114, 136, 165; Will, 112.
Wolstenholme, Sir John, 196.
Wriothesley, Henry, 3d Earl of Southampton, and last Treasurer of the Virginia Corporation, 15, 16, 28, 32, 33, 36-38, 42, 44-47, 62, 71, 90, 91, 114, 129, 133, 136, 147; Thomas, 4th Earl of Southampton, 102, 133, 134, 136, 139. See Southampton House, and Titchfield.
Wrong. See Historic wrong.
Wrote, Samuel, 35, 196.
Wroth, John, 35, 222; Sir Thomas, 196.
Wyatt, Sir Francis, 35, 41, 92, 93, 97, 102, 104, 127, 161.
Wythe, George, 144.

Yeardley, Sir George, 18, 20, 29, 92, 93, 114, 126, 127, 162, 225.

Zane, Isaac, 139, 140.
Zuñiga, Don Pedro de, 30.

The Riverside Press
Electrotyped and printed by H. O. Houghton & Co.
Cambridge, Mass., U. S. A.

www.ingramcontent.com/pod-product-compliance
Lightning Source LLC
Chambersburg PA
CBHW071424150426
43191CB00008B/1031